CLAUDE-NICOLAS LEDOUX

ANTHONY VIDLER

CLAUDE-NICOLAS LEDOUX

ARCHITECTURE AND UTOPIA IN THE ERA OF THE FRENCH REVOLUTION

Birkhäuser – Publishers for Architecture
Basel · Berlin · Boston

GRAPHIC DESIGN: Sylvie Milliet
LAYOUT OF THE ENGLISH EDITION: Alexandra Zöller
COVER DESIGN: Jean-Marc Barrier,
adapted for the English edition by Muriel Comby
EDITORIAL COORDINATION: Chloë Jarry
EDITOR FOR THE ENGLISH EDITION,
TRANSLATION OF CAPTIONS: Michael Wachholz
ICONOGRAPHIC RESEARCH: Françoise Carp and Isabelle Sallé

This book is also available in a German language edition
(ISBN-10: 3-7643-7484-5; ISBN-13: 978-3-7643-7484-6)

Original title "LEDOUX", written by Anthony Vidler,
published by Editions Hazan, 2005
© Editions Hazan, Paris, 2005
© Saline Royale d'Arc-et-Senans, 2005

A CIP catalogue record for this book is available from the Library of
Congress, Washington D.C., USA

Bibliographic information published by Die Deutsche Bibliothek
Die Deutsche Bibliothek lists this publication in the Deutsche
Nationalbibliografie; detailed bibliographic data is available in the
Internet at <http://dnb.ddb.de>.

© 2006 Birkhäuser – Publishers for Architecture, P.O.Box 133,
CH-4010 Basel, Switzerland
Part of Springer Science + Business Media
Printed on acid-free paper produced from chlorine-free pulp. TCF ∞

Printed in Singapore
ISBN-10 3-7643-7485-3
ISBN-13 978-3-7643-7485-3

www.birkhauser.ch
9 8 7 6 5 4 3 2 1

CONTENTS

As critics from the eighteenth century to the present have pointed out, Ledoux's mercurial and omnivorous architectural personality has opened his design and writing to endless interpretation; one could indeed write a history of architectural history from the vantage point of Ledoux's reception over the last two centuries. Equally important has been his reception by architects, whether preparing the way for the geometrical exercises of Napoleon's *bâtiments civils*, studied as a forerunner of abstract modernism by the Russian Constructivists, the French Purists, the Italian Neo-Rationalists, seen as a suitable megalomanical monumentalist for the Third Reich, adopted as a figural expressionist by Postmodernists, or now revived as a model of late Modernism. His personal influence on individual architects from Ivan Leonidov, Le Corbusier, Philip Johnson, Louis Kahn, Aldo Rossi, Michael Graves, to Jean Nouvel, among many others, has been freely admitted. Which is to say that, throughout his posthumous life, Ledoux has acted as a bell-wether for modernity in architecture. His idiosyncratic combination of geometrical purity, iconographical inventiveness, and Enlightenment ideology, has made him, in fact, the very prototype of the modern, if not avant-garde, reformist architect.

In re-reading this essay, first written in 1985-86, I find that there is little I would change in my overall interpretation of the life and work of Claude-Nicolas Ledoux.[1] My general argument is that Ledoux was less the exception than the rule in the newly established professionalism of the late eighteenth century; that his quasi-utopian enthusiasm for raising aesthetic expression to a social art, for the beliefs in progress of the *philosophes*, while sympathizing with the "return to origins" of Rousseau, for the technological innovations promoted by the *Encyclopédie* and its contributors was common to a number of professions – including engineering, medicine, jurisprudence – and if Ledoux stands out among his architectural peers, it is more because he took the Enlightenment at its word so to speak, and was less inhibited by architectural tradition in seeking to apply the aesthetic experiments of his literary peers to the invention of new forms.

He was at the same time deeply respectful of the tradition of French classicism; and, as I have come to appreciate, even more determined to return to the ideal city principles of the French and Italian Renaissance. A large number of his apparent innovations in style and iconography, indeed, can be traced to his spirit of revival, rather than to any desire to shock or disturb the foundations of the Ancien Régime. Thus I continue to believe that he is best interpreted aesthetically *and* historically, from the standpoint of a history that understands architecture as a social, economic, and aesthetic practice, where design takes on a complex role, at once emblem and instrument, spectacle and shelter, ideal and

6

Following double page:
Saline d'Arc-et-Senans,
view of the eastern semi-circular arc.

EDITION

utopia. It is in this mode that Ledoux operated, with all the self-consciousness and pioneering sensibility of the newly minted professional in the service of a still nascent state, and on behalf of a society conceived according to the principles laid out by Diderot, Condillac, and Rousseau.

In the seventeen years since this essay was written, beside that of my own monograph, two major works have added to our understanding of Ledoux. In 1991 Michel Gallet published a hundred previously unknown Ledoux engravings found by Georges Fréchet in the Bibliothèque Historique de la Ville de Paris in 1983. With a preface by Monique Mosser, and a summary of Ledoux's life and work by Gallet, this volume was entitled *Architecture de Ledoux. Inédits pour un Tome III*. These engravings demonstrate Ledoux's historical eclecticism in the rediscovered projects for Maisons de Campagne, one similar to British architects of the day, such as Robert Adam in his "baronial" house designs, but suppressed by Daniel Ramée in his mid-nineteenth century edition of *L'Architecture*, perhaps to support his own thesis of a rigorously neo-classic and geometrically pure Ledoux. More recently, Daniel Rabreau has offered a presentation of Ledoux's aesthetics, a study that develops a fresh interpretation of the artistic values of his work. I have taken account of these and other more recent works in the corrections, revisions, and additions to the present text.

I have benefited from correspondence with André Corboz on the foundation of Versoix; from discussions with Hubert Damisch on the "Kantian" Ledoux; from the experience of conceiving and designing the installation for the permanent exhibition of models of Ledoux's work in the Saline Royale d'Arc-et-Senans in 1989; from the work of Antoine Picon on the formation of the École des Ponts et Chaussées and the relations between architects and engineers in the late eighteenth century, and most especially from the generosity of Paul Turner, who provided a clue to the source of Ledoux's utopian imagination in the Renaissance treatise *Hypnerotomachia Poliphili* that has led to an expansion of the last chapter. I have added a number of new illustrations, including a selection of the recently discovered engravings, and some now classic photographic studies by Georges Fessy. I will always be indebted to the support and firm friendship of Richard Edwards during his tenure as Director of the Fondation Ledoux, to the continuing support of the present Director, Jean Dedolin, to Jean-François Barrielle and Chloé Jarry of Editions Hazan, and to the editor, Andreas Müller, whose idea it was to publish the first English edition of this book.

Anthony Vidler,
New York, November 2005

INTRODUCTION

"Are we fallen into such misery that we are absolutely obliged to admire the tollgates of Paris?"

Victor Hugo[2]

As critics from the eighteenth century to the present have pointed out, Ledoux's mercurial and omnivorous architectural personality has opened his design and writing to endless interpretation; one could indeed write a history of architectural history from the vantage point of Ledoux's reception over the last two centuries.

In his own lifetime, Ledoux, at first recognised as a brilliant but wayward designer, was in quick order reviled as a ruinous architect, a megalomaniac and an enemy of classicism. Quatremère de Quincy accused him of having submitted architecture to "all kinds of torture," and this aesthetic disapproval was joined to political disgrace after the Revolution.[3] The former architect of Madame du Barry and faithful servant of the Ferme Générale, or royal tax farm, who attempted to "imprison" the population of Paris by a fiscal wall entered through *barrières*, or tollgates, found little sympathy for his pre-Revolutionary projects of industrial and rural reform. Quatremère de Quincy's verdict was, for different reasons, echoed by Victor Hugo in the 1830s as he accused the architects of the late eighteenth century of having reduced architecture to mere geometry, the "bony skeleton of an emaciated invalid;" the tollgates seemed to him the worst examples of a modern architecture unworthy to stand beside that of the Middle Ages. His was only one of the voices condemning Ledoux's architecture under the July Monarchy. Léon Vaudoyer, son of one of Ledoux's colleagues and emulators, invented the caustic epithet "architecture parlante" to characterise the most pictogrammatic of his designs.[4] These commonplaces were repeated, with few exceptions, through to the 1920s, when a new appreciation of abstraction rediscovered Ledoux as the forerunner of Le Corbusier, in the formulation of the Viennese art historian Emil Kaufmann: *Von Ledoux bis Le Corbusier*.[5] Ledoux was now seen as the eponymous hero of modernism, even as he was counted among those architects of the Enlightenment to have prepared a "revolution" in architecture equivalent to that in politics after 1789. Certainly, as Kaufmann himself recognised, Ledoux was no political revolutionary; but the formal transformations and utopian aspirations of his work seemed, in the late 1920s, to have anticipated the "autonomous" forms of the emerging bourgeois state. Like Cassirer, preoccupied with the troubling dichotomy between the objective reason of Kant and the emphatic individuality of Rousseau, Kaufmann found in Ledoux a rich subject for study at a moment when the ideals of social democracy were being attacked from the emotional appeals of the Third Reich.

That Hitler's architects found inspiration in the inflated monumentality of neo-classicism while denouncing modernism as decadent; that the former National Socialist art historian Hans Sedlmayr would rejoin the attack on Ledoux, this time as the evil genius of the world's "loss of centre;"[6] that Ledoux would, in the late 1960s, be appropriated on behalf of a renewed utopian socialism; and that, in the 1980s, he would be the much imitated idol of postmodernism; and more recently, the forerunner of modernism once again – all these shifts have merely reinforced confusion in the interpretation of his work. They have also contributed to the sense of his extraordinary and protean inventiveness that at once synthesised the ideals of Enlightenment in architecture, and projected them into a utopian vision that still has resonance. Recent art historians have tended to concentrate on one or more of his multiple traits. Thus some have emphasised his "visionary" characteristics, seeking occult and mystical meanings in his geometries. Others have preferred to see him as heir to the aristocratic iconographers and decorators of earlier periods; as a theatrical producer of aesthetic effects; or, alternatively, as a kind of French Bentham, anticipating the panopticism of a later industrial age. Of all the historians who have considered Ledoux, Michel Gallet alone has worked painstakingly in the archives to situate the architect within the real conditions of late eighteenth-century practice.[7]

Following double page:
Perspective view
of the city
of Chaux.
From: *L'Architecture...*,
Plate 15.

Against these "aesthetics of reception," however, must be posed another Ledoux: one who, while embodying many of these divergent traits, was more an architect of his time and a believer in the Enlightenment than many scholars have wished to admit. This Ledoux was marked by his position as a "self-made man," rising from the rural petit-bourgeoisie through talent and achieving, sooner than many of his peers, a fully-fledged and ambitious vision of the role of the modern architect. From this perspective, Ledoux emerges as an entirely comprehensible figure, the direct product in architecture of the moral and educational theory and practice of the mid-century *philosophes*, and more precisely, of the circle around the *Encyclopédie*. His ideals were the shared commonplaces of a generation responsive to Diderot and his collaborators, and he drew readily if eclectically from the theories of *philosophes*, agronomists, economists, and writers committed to the reform of traditional institutions and social practices.

If Ledoux's ideological affiliations are clear, and easily decipherable in the allusive and amphibological text of his book, the idiosyncratic qualities of his architecture, built and projected, are less susceptible to analysis. Thus, while he shared the reaction of many of his contemporaries against the vegetal excesses of the rococo, his particular version of the "return to antiquity" in the 1770s, noted by historians from Louis Hautecœur to Michel Gallet, avoided both the eclectic play of the Piranesian ruin motifs of Legeay, de Wailly, and Hubert Robert, and the increasing "Greek" historicism of antiquarians like David Le Roy and Quatremère de Quincy.[8] Similarly, while his Palladianism, like that of Brongniart, Bélanger, and Chalgrin, had its roots in England, his effortless absorption of forms and motifs from the English Renaissance and baroque – Inigo Jones, Wren, Vanbrugh, Hawksmoor, and Adam – resisted any strict allegiance to Venetian mannerism.[9]

These particularities may, on one level, be explained by the circumstances of Ledoux's education; without independent means or rich patron he was unable to follow the traditional route to Rome; his experience of "antiquity," insofar as it existed, was largely confined to French examples, even as his classicism looked to equally French models from the seventeenth century on. If indeed he ever visited England, as Michel Gallet surmises, it was probably late in his career, a confirmation of sources already tapped. Trained as an engraver, his architectural knowledge was for the most part derived almost entirely from engravings: from Colen Campbell's *Vitruvius Britannicus*, Jacques-François Blondel's *Architecture française* and from the plates of the *Encyclopédie*.[10] This is no doubt why his architecture, more than that of Blondel's other students, seems at once abstract and essentially theoretical; freely assembled of representations and images of buildings, its geometrical reduction at once a product of the engraver's technique and an instrument of combinatorial invention. His work is didactic in the same vein as the plates for Diderot's *Encyclopédie*, analytical and synthetic at the same time.[11]

This is where Kaufmann rightly sensed a proto-modernist Ledoux in an architecture formed not out of a replication of historical precedent but out of the transformational properties of three-dimensional geometry – the art of representing stone cutting, called stereotomy – producing infinitely varied effects of solid massing on the exterior and rich interpenetrations of volumes in the interior. And while it may be historically risky to compare Ledoux to Le Corbusier once more, it is nevertheless true that both architects developed their formal systems out of the interplay of narrative and structure: in the case of Le Corbusier in the interweaving of the *promenade architecturale* and the properties of primary solids; in that of Ledoux, in an exploitation of all the emblematic power of axial routes combined with the systematic coherence of variations on the nine-square plan. A less anachronistic analogy, and one that would have pleased Ledoux himself, would be to the ritual movements of Gluck's operas and the symmetrical elegance of Mozart's symphonies.

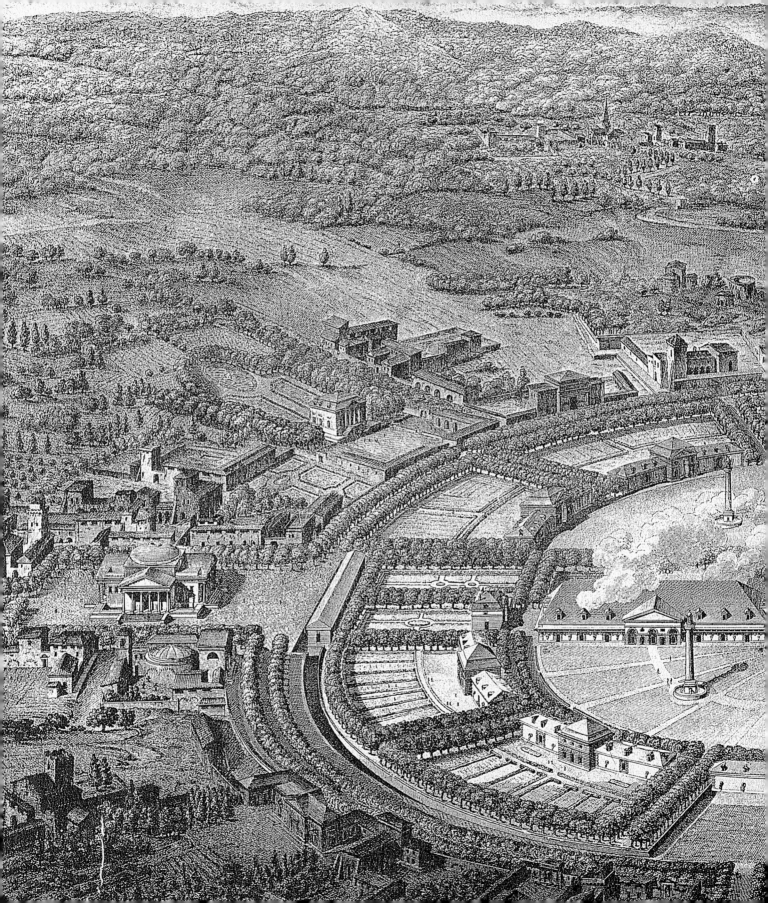

CLASSICISM

1. CLASSICAL MAXIMS

"For the moralists you should open up Cicero's dialogues on old age, friendship, and the nature of the gods; in this way you will substitute the real for the false and encourage the practice of all the virtues. For the farmer you should open up the treasures of Columella, the *Works and Days* of Hesiod, and the *Georgics* of the poet of Mantua, already Gallicised by our own Virgil [the Abbé Delille]. But where will all these efforts lead? Where indeed! They will familiarise you with the celebrated men of letters, and those divine minds who guide my own audacity." [148][1]

Claude-Nicolas Ledoux was born in the village of Dormans, Marne, on 27th March 1736.[2] His father, Claude Ledoux, a merchant, and his mother, Françoise Dominot, were, if not poor, of modest means and Ledoux was fortunate, after attending the parish school, to obtain a scholarship from the diocese of Soissons to study in Paris. He was to remember the first thirteen years of his life in the countryside of Champagne with affection and nostalgia for its solid rural honesty. His professional career was always to be linked to the reform of agriculture, and the re-settlement of society in natural surroundings became a preoccupation of his later years. When, as an old man, he dreamed of a utopia in Franche-Comté, it was to be filled with images of a lost childhood, juxtaposed with the rustic festivals,

Louis Michel
Van Loo,
*Dénis Diderot,
writer*, 18th century.
Oil on canvas,
81 x 65 cm.
Paris,
Musée du Louvre.

seasonal occupations and the artisanal practices of village life. Concerned, like Rousseau, with the proper bases for a natural morality in education and upbringing, Ledoux found in his own upbringing a model for that of society in general. Despite his later distrust of academic formulae, Ledoux's three years at the Collège de Beauvais in Paris, from 1749 to 1753, introduced him to a world that he was never, in imagination at least, to leave: that of the classics, ancient and modern and of the sciences of progress and reform; it also provided him with the skills of a geometer, and the company of other upwardly mobile professionals and their future patrons, private and public.[3] In this college of Jansenist foundation, Ledoux lived in common with the masters and fellow scholars, wearing the obligatory blue and white robes and acquiring a life-long taste for Greek and Latin poetry and rhetoric. The effectiveness of the didactic method devised by Charles Rollin, which depended on a series of exemplary "morceaux choisies" extracted from the great books of history to exemplify moral and social virtues, was attested to by Ledoux's continuing and inveterate sciolism. His writing and his designs were to be larded with classical references and half-remembered quotations. On the evidence of his magnum opus, *L'Architecture considérée sous le rapport de l'art, des moeurs, et de la législation*, published in 1804 two years before his death, his reading was wide if conventional: Homer, Plato, Virgil, Ovid, and Horace were his poetic models; Plutarch, Pliny, Tacitus and Caesar provided his anecdotic knowledge of history; Cicero, Aristotle and a host of lesser Roman writers furnished a knowledge of *l'ancienne rhétorique*; Hesiod, Xenophon and Columella were cited for their teachings on rural life and agriculture. To this, a few of the "moderns" contributed by the Jansenists, were added: Racine and Pascal were seen as the twin supports of classicism and metaphysical enquiry; Fénelon's *Télémaque* supplied the figure of Mentor for the reforming architect instructing a prince; Fontenelle's *Entretiens sur la pluralité des mondes* anticipated Ledoux's reveries of the future; La Fontaine's *Fables* and La Bruyère's *Caractères* evoked parables and physiognomical images.[4]

This "utopia of the schoolroom," where history was taught without tears and where the golden sun of antiquity coloured nature and art alike, furnished the context for much of Ledoux's work, real and ideal. Classical precedent was not so much followed as it was used to legitimate his own inventions: etymology authorised the tollgates or *barrières* of Paris to be re-named "Propylaea," [16]; neologisms offered the potential of creating and naming entirely new institutions – the "Oikéma" or House of Pleasure [199-204], the "Panaréthéon" or House of Virtue [309-314], the "Pacifère" or House of Peace [113] – a technique also used by Rétif de la Bretonne and later by

Charles Fourier. Classical references similarly provided precedents for unprecedented or unfamiliar designs: the example of "Roman charity" was adopted for a new system of poor relief in the Market of Chaux [165]; a shocking sexual licence from Horace was criticised by Plato [202]; appropriate allegories were selected to characterise new building-types; maxims and precepts were engraved on the walls of monuments for popular instruction. These lexical tactics were reinforced by the exercises in style and rhetoric repeated incessantly in the classroom and taken by Ledoux as the foundations of his design method. Thus Ledoux elevated the commonplace routines of writing and speech – transposition, précis, amplification, and figurative discourse – into architectural procedures. Transposition was the means by which everyday surroundings were endowed with exotic aura; the countryside of Franche-Comté, for example, was at once seen through the conventional descriptions of the Roman campagna, and in the poetic guise of Arcadia. Amplification was a favourite trick, as Ledoux used telescopic and microscopic vision to make small things large, microcosms to macrocosms. The architect, he held, "will provide for the smallest object that which the largest admits." [16-17] But figural invention was his most absorbing pastime, as "the figurative style "[16] was applied to every subject and programme, not simply in the text of *L'Architecture*, but as literally

applied to the buildings, themselves conceived as rhetorical periods. Allegories and emblems were attached to walls in the form of bas-reliefs, and in many cases, the entire building was envisaged as a figurative translation of its function, like a three-dimensional illustration to the *Traité des tropes* of Dumarsais, the standard book of rhetoric for the later eighteenth century.[5]

These early *exercices de style* were given aesthetic focus in the ten years after 1753 by Ledoux's experiences, first as an apprentice engraver where, as Jacques Cellerier, his friend and biographer noted, he engraved battle scenes to defray his expenses, and then in the École des Arts of Jacques-François Blondel.[6] His formation as engraver contrasted with other would-be "artist-architects" of the period – Etienne-Louis Boullée, who considered himself a painter, or Charles de Wailly, for example – and explains Ledoux's insistence on the constant revision of his plates, following the model of Piranesi, as well as his self-conscious emulation of the plates of the *Encyclopédie* for those of *L'Architecture*, where page by page, a perspective vignette surmounts an "analytical" dissection of the object in plan, section and elevation.[7] This training equally influenced his distinctly individual handling of line, three-dimensional solids, light and shade with the burin rather than with the brush.

His architectural formation with Blondel, that also no doubt included periods in the ateliers of Pierre

Contant d'Ivry and Louis-François Trouard, was, despite his later irritation with the pedantic "professeur," decisive, both as an introduction to architecture considered philosophically by Blondel, the contributor to the *Encyclopédie*, and as a formulation of the designer's task in terms of the gamut of social institutions, carefully described in Blondel's lectures according to their proper *distribution* and *caractère*.[8] From Blondel's lectures, Ledoux absorbed the standard list of academic keywords, repeating them in the introduction to his *L'Architecture* nearly half a century later. Some were inherited from Vitruvius as interpreted by Claude Perrault: health (*salubrité*) order (*ordonnance*), symmetry (*symétrie*), proportion (*proportion*), fitness or suitability (*convenance*), and propriety (*bienséance*). Others had been given special significance by seventeenth-century rationalism: unity (*unité*), severity (*severité*), judgement (*jugement*), reasoning (*raisonnement*), and method (*méthode*). Others still had been taken from the classical tradition, but given new force by eighteenth-century sensationalist aesthetics: character (*caractère*), contrast (*contraste*), variety (*variété*). Some referred to an emerging consciousness of empirical constraints – disposition, arrangement (*distribution*), need (*besoin*).[9]

Of them all, the most important concept for Blondel and his students was that of *caractère*. It was under this rubric that Blondel discussed and his students explored, the formation of building-types, public and private, symbolic and utilitarian. Blondel's celebrated admonition, repeated in various forms as the introduction to all his student programmes, was learned by rote: "All the different kinds of works that belong to architecture should bear the imprint of the intended purpose of each building, all must possess a character that determines their general form and that announces the building for what it is."[10] This call for proper characterisation, as the continuing experiments of Ledoux's generation demonstrated, was no simple academic commonplace in an age where individual and social tastes were gradually replacing hitherto "absolute" standards, and where the emergence of a host of new social and institutional needs forced the architect to improvise the invention of new building-types. Blondel was here drawing on a more general theory of characterisation, as developed in the natural histories of Buffon and Linneaus, the enquiries of linguists into the origins and nature of language and signs, and theatrical and painterly theories of gesture and expression.[11] In architecture, the sense of characterisation was, as in science, divided between a study of suitable expression – the signs of character – and an analysis of organisation, or distribution – the constitution of character; between that is, in Michel Foucault's terms, "a theory of the mark and a theory of the organism."[12] It was Ledoux's ambition to overcome this eventually fatal division of architecture between need and representation in such a way that the building became, so to speak, a transparent sign of its own purpose.

The problem had been stated bluntly enough by d'Alembert in the *Discours préliminaire* to the *Encyclopédie*, where, in a deceptively simple formulation, he had defined architecture as "that art, born of necessity and perfected by luxury … that, being elevated by degrees from huts to palaces, is, to the eyes of the philosopher, if one can say it thus, only the embellished mask of one of our greatest needs."[13] While the idea of the gradual evolution of architecture from cottages to palaces was common enough in classical theory, that of the *masque embelli* was not, and took on special significance in the discourse of a thinker, such as d'Alembert, who stood firmly against any forms of dissimulation or mystifying rhetoric. The proscription of "masks," part of the general campaign of the *philosophes* against superstition and error, was illustrated in Nicolas Cochin's frontispiece to the *Encyclopédie* where the figure of *vérité* stood beneath a temple surrounded by the muses of the arts and sciences and about to be stripped of her traditional veil of *pudeur* by the blinding light of Reason. Rousseau had pointed to the dire moral consequences of a civilisation that revelled in masks of every kind, looking back with nostalgia to an age when all characters were announced at a glance; Diderot had defined *vérité* in painting as "the expression suitable to the character of each thing," and called for a drama of honest passions.[14]

In this context d'Alembert's proposition would seem paradoxical: architecture as the art of embellishing need was, as a mask, founded on a false if not immoral principle. The question was widely debated. Pierre Patte, also a student of Blondel and publisher of his course of lectures after his death, some years later replied directly to d'Alembert by proposing that the solution lay in *distribution*, that is in functional accommodation;[15] others, like the Abbé Laugier, would return architecture to its origins in structural integrity;[16] others again sought to develop a language of forms that would act as unambiguous expressions of character. Ledoux, registering Rousseau's strictures, and similarly nostalgic for primitive language, tried on the one hand to elide the distinctions between cottages and palaces by giving the former the status of architecture, and on the other, to invent a language of characters, searching, so to speak, for *la vérité en architecture*.

Adapted from Maurice Quentin de La Tour, *Jean Le Rond d'Alembert*, 18th century.

Oil on canvas, 63 x 52 cm. Châteaux de Versailles et de Trianon.

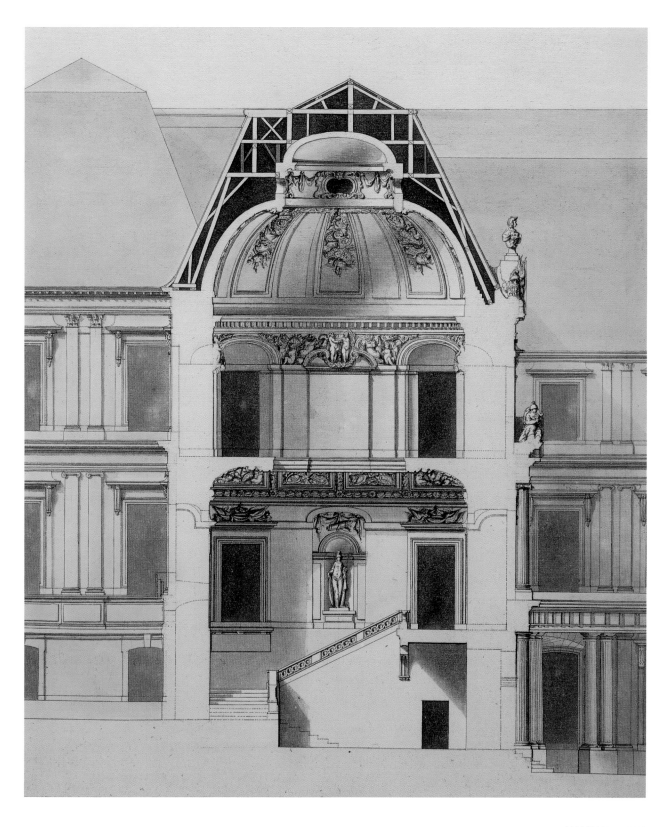

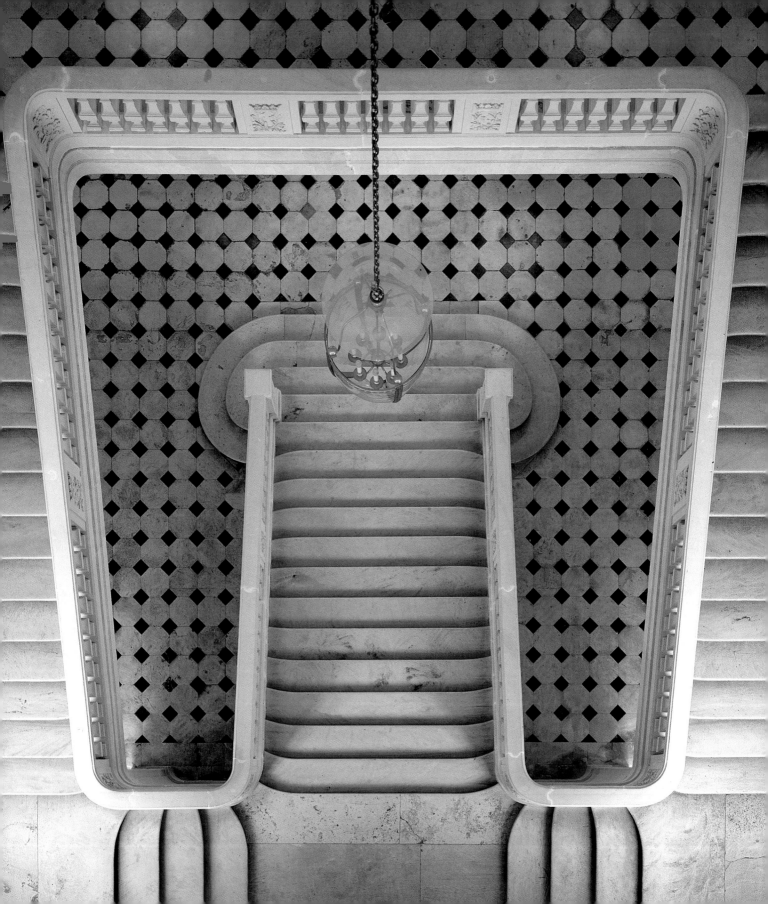

2. EMBLEMS OF NOBILITY

"When I speak of the nobility, I wish to recall that inalienable value transmitted to the heroes of this country by the race of the Caesars, a value that cannot be effaced by the hand of time." [212]

Ledoux's sympathy with the aesthetic ideals of the Encyclopedists, and his identification with their views on the reform of agriculture and industry were never extended to embrace the more radical political consequences of philosophic doctrines. Still less was Ledoux, whether practising architect or utopian dreamer, a radical revolutionary in the sense of the Revolutionaries of the early 1790s. Nor did he, despite his own modest origins, seek to overturn the established hierarchies in society by substituting a pyramid based on talent, as Henri de Saint-Simon was later to suggest. In Ledoux's ideal state, the Ancien Régime would remain for the most part intact, with its castes of nobles, its three estates, its corporations and institutions, its *parlements* and its monarchy. The only change he sought, one entirely consonant with his aesthetic vision, was that each member of society should be invested with architectural recognition, from the rural peasant to the prince, appropriate to his character or to that of his role. And the determination of such character was to be accomplished according to the equally powerful law of origins, with each metier, each function, each estate

Left page:
Château de
Bénouville,
view of the
staircase.

Above:
Château de
Bénouville,
detail of
the columns.

Hôtel d'Uzès, identically reassembled panelling in the salon. Paris, Musée Carnavalet.

Right page: Château de Bénouville, detail of the facade.

traced back to its natural authority and form. Ledoux himself never hid his ambitions for ennoblement, and his early taste for military exploits, chivalric tales and classical emblems conformed exactly to those of his first patrons, for the most part younger nobles of the robe and the sword, anxious to prove their titles in what François Furet has termed "a kind of defensive exasperation ... a genealogical fever that a contemporary termed 'title mania'."[1] Thus the Marquis de Montesquiou and the Prince de Bauffremont traced their line back to Clovis, as did another of Ledoux's patrons, the Prince de Montmorency, joining a new interest in French history to a firm belief in original legitimacy against the ubiquitous trade in title-granting.

Ledoux's first recorded independent commission, the Café Godeau, or "Café Militaire" of 1762, nicely exhibited his aristocratic concerns to a fashionable clientele of veterans and officers a year before the end of the Seven Years War. The *salle de café*, now re-mounted in the Musée Carnavalet, was a textbook illustration of his classical education, adopting a fiction, perhaps adapted from Caesar's *Commentaries* as a background to the officers' sociability. In the words of Élie Fréron, for once an appreciative critic, Ledoux had imagined "that the officers, retiring from combat, find a spot for relaxation, bundle their spears, binding them up with the laurels of victory and crowning them picturesquely with their helmets. The resulting effect is of twelve triumphal columns around the room, repeated to infinity through the magic of the mirrors."[2] This decor announced many of Ledoux's future preoccupations: a narrative story that gave authority to the invention; an idealisation of contemporary sociability by means of antique reference; the use of emblems strongly carved in bas-relief against smooth surfaces, to ensure legibility; an aesthetic of contrast and elemental simplicity; the visual play with infinity, and, finally, a concern with a return to origins.[3] Here, as against the structural origins of architecture propounded by the Abbé Laugier, where architecture was reduced to a combination of its three major parts, column, architrave and pediment, Ledoux sug-

gests an architecture founded on the twin bases of rhetoric and sociability. In this primitive tent constructed out of the symbols of warrior life, Ledoux anticipated his later utopia, built with the aid of a *rhétorique restreinte* and decorated with an assemblage of motifs drawn from antiquity attached to the otherwise bare walls of its monuments.

This combination of noble attributes and a simplified classicism was developed by Ledoux, in the first ten years of his practice, for clients related by marriage and friendship and eager to be flattered by elaborate armorial devices, historical pedigrees in stone, and simple but elegant salons.[4] Trophies, triumphal arches, free-standing monumental columns, antique torsos, naval and military symbols, and statues of mythical ancestors decorated his houses for Fermiers Généraux, members of the *parlements*, nobles of the sword and the robe, in town and country. Of these, the gate of the Hôtel d'Uzès and the statues of the *constables* of Montmorency were the most striking. Within these grand houses, following the model of the Café Militaire, Ledoux decorated the *salons de compagnie* with exquisite panelling carved and gilded in low relief. That of the Hôtel d'Uzès, carved by Joseph Métivier, returned to the allegory of the café, creating the illusion of a gilded forest, with trees, festooned with emblems of the arts and war, rising directly from the floor and reflected in mirrored panels.

The decorative scheme of the Hôtel Montmorency, also by Métivier, displayed muses, alternating with cupids and vases around the circular salon. Perhaps reflecting the Montmorency family's close connection to freemasonry, the symbolism of compasses, squares, globes and staff of Mercury was pronounced.

The style of these first *hôtels* mingled a return to French classical sources – the rear wall of the garden court in the Hôtel d'Hallwyl, for example, was a direct citation from the decorative

schema of the Fontaine de Médicis in the Jardin du Luxembourg – with a simplified form of Palladian planning. Thus the Pavilion Hocquart, with its central circular dining room, domed and top-lit, and its roughly square plan entered through pedimented Ionic porches was based loosely on Palladio's Villa Rotunda; the Hôtel Montmorency, also planned within a square, elegantly developed the sequence of reception rooms and main stair along a diagonal in order to respond to the corner site. In the countryside Ledoux was able to extend

Café Militaire,
wood-carved panel.
Paris,
Musée Carnavalet.

Left page:
Château de
Bénouville,
staircase.

this "English" manner to the grounds, outbuildings and gardens of great estates, indulging his taste for the picturesque, also derived from English examples, notably at the Château de Maupertuis for the Marquis de Montesquiou.[5] Here, Ledoux not only re-built the family chateau, embellishing it with Ionic colonnades, but supplied designs for the orangery, a pheasantry forming a small temple in the woods, a pavilion for the agricultural guards – the celebrated spherical house published by Daniel Ramée – the layout of the park itself, and numerous outbuildings.[6] A rustic entrance fountain built out of the natural stone of the region completed the composition of this estate where Ledoux was to meet many of the influential patrons, artists and writers of the day, including the painter Hubert Robert, the poet Delille and the architect Brongniart, all with shared mutual interests in agricultural reform, the theatre and freemasonry.[7]

In 1770, two commissions, readily associated in the popular mind by the notoriety of their clients – two of the most celebrated courtesans of the day – sealed Ledoux's ascending reputation as an architect of fashion. For Mlle. Guimard, former first dancer at the Comédie-Française and later a dancer at the Opéra, Ledoux built an *hôtel* in the rapidly expanding quarter of the Chaussée d'Antin, together with a private theatre for the intimate performances that evoked the aura of delicious scandal enjoyed by Edmund de Goncourt over a century later.[8] For Madame du Barry, newly installed mistress of Louis XV, Ledoux constructed what Goncourt called a "palais-boudoir" in the gardens of Louveciennes next to Versailles.[9] The voyeurism of late-nineteenth century nostalgia, however, has tended to obscure the architectural significance of these pavilions that at once demonstrated Ledoux's capacity to produce an almost theatrical synthesis of the decorative arts and architecture, and provided, in the context of the Guimard theatre, an initial opportunity to explore the complex relations between audience and scene in the geometries of the auditorium. Both pavilions, further, disposed their reception rooms, each decorated and individually shaped in plan, in a masterly sequence and composition within the simple cubic envelope of the

whole. The decorative schemes of both commissions were immediately recognised as innovative and appropriate for their owners. For the Maison Guimard, Ledoux modelled the interior on the delightfully erotic novel of a "seductive house," *La petite maison* by Blondel's friend, Jean-François de Bastide, with its mirrored dining room painted like a forest; for Madame du Barry, he designed a splendid table setting, with three golden temples in the centre, and a painted cycle (later rejected by du Barry herself) by Fragonard that depicted the amorous life of the *patronne*.[10] These commissions naturally brought Ledoux into contact with an expanded patronage. At the private performances in Guimard's theatre, he met the Duc de Chartres, later a client for one of the Parisian tollgates, Frederick II, Landgrave of Hesse-Cassel, who called Ledoux to his capital in 1776, and Joseph II, brother of Marie-Antoinette, later to subscribe to the publication of *L'Architecture*. At Louveciennes, Ledoux received a private audience with Louis XV, who expressed himself satisfied with the proportions of the columns. As the favourite architect of du Barry, Ledoux

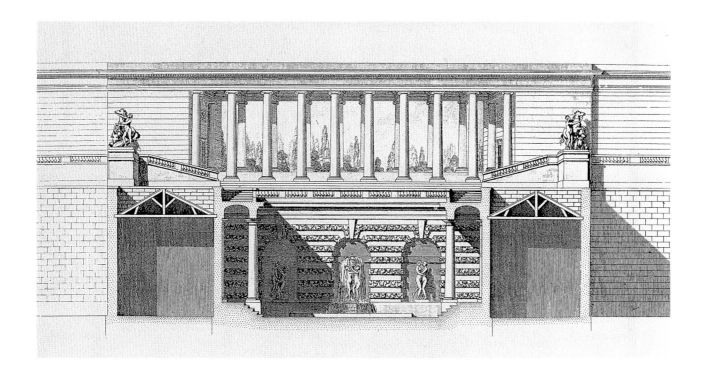

shared in the rewards of a cultural politics that was aimed at rivalling Madame de Pompadour's control over the arts. An unsuccessful candidate for the Académie d'Architecture in 1767, Ledoux was finally elected in 1773 in the wake of Marigny's unseating as Directeur Générale des Bâtiments du Roi and his replacement by the opportunistic minister of finance, the Abbé Terray; a scornful critic wrote, "The Director of Buildings wrote to the company [of the Academy] that Madame du Barry wanted Ledoux to be elected, and he was."[11] Madame du Barry herself continued to employ Ledoux in the construction of her carriage house and stables at Versailles, in the planning for vast palaces at Louveciennes and Paris, and, after her exile in 1774, for a more modest chateau at Saint-Vrain near Arpajon.

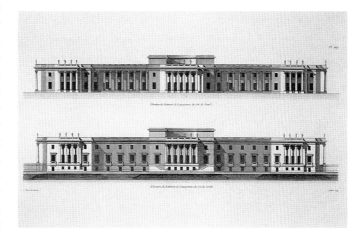

Left page and above: Hôtel d'Hallwyl. Elevation from rue de Michel-le-Comte; section C-D. From: *L'Architecture...*, Ramée edition, Plates 158 and 158 bottom.

Building at Louveciennes, entrance elevation, garden elevation. From: *L'Architecture...*, Ramée edition, Plate 171.

Following double page: House of Mlle. Guimard in the Chausée d'Antin. From: *L'Architecture...*, Ramée edition, Plate 176.

3. PUBLIC ADMINISTRATION

"In those days architects also built bridges." [45]

During these ten years, as the meticulous scholarship of Michel Gallet has demonstrated, Ledoux also worked for the Service des Eaux et Forêts, designing and providing estimates for an entire range of small rural buildings in the Haute-Marne, Haute-Saône, Yonne and Aube: repairs to presbyteries and sacristies, schoolhouses and cemeteries, additions to and reconstructions of parish churches, the paving of roads, wells, fountains, horse-troughs and wash-houses, as well as a number of simple bridges over local streams and rivers.[1] In its range and architectural style, this repertoire of modest rural structures anticipated Ledoux's later projects for a more comprehensive *architecture rurale* and brought him into contact with the corps of engineers in the recently established Ponts et Chaussées. The earliest of the churches, at Rolampont, established the elements of his style: a nave and aisles vaulted in flattened segmental arches, carried on square piers with corbels fashioned out of Doric triglyphs; a porch with pediment and single arched door set into the cut stone facade; a square bell-tower with corner pilasters surmounted by the bell-shaped roof typical of Franche-Comté. The most elaborate was at Cruzy-le-Châtel, where nave and aisles were vaulted in semi-circular arches on square piers, again in simplified Doric, while the porch, flanked

Left page:
Prégibert Bridge,
near Rolampont
(Haute-Marne).

Above:
Salt granary
of Compiègne,
facade.

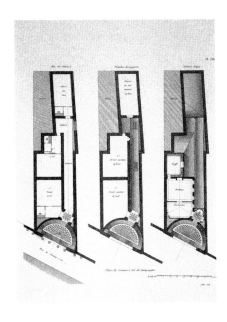

Salt granary of
Compiègne, plan.
From: *L'Architecture...*,
Ramée edition,
Plate 106.

Below:
Church Saint-Didier
in Roche
(Haute-Saône).

Right page:
Church Saint-Pierre-
aux-Liens in Rolampont
(Haute-Marne).

Following double page:
North-west view of
the Saline Royale,
view of the
surrounding wall.

by double Doric pilasters was crowned by a pediment in full relief, with triglyphs and metopes.
Equally significant in the formation of Ledoux's
"public style," were the bridges, especially those
near Rolampont and Marac, exemplary of the
reform of engineering aesthetics taught by Perronet at the École des Ponts et Chaussées.[2] Their
flattened arches prefigured not only future
bridges projected by Ledoux, such as the combination bridge and *abreuvoir* for the École Rurale
de Meilhan of 1793 [Ramée, II, Pl. 288], but also
heralded his favourite device for visual framing
– architecture viewed from beneath a bridge –
a motif adopted by a number of Piranesi's followers and by Hubert Robert in particular.[3]
Ledoux was well aware of the aesthetic implica-
tions of these simple engineering forms: "the
principal beauty of a bridge consists in the purity of its lines," [47] he wrote; at the same time
he was conscious of functional concerns, notably
the problem of erosion of the piles, studied by
Perronet and by the engineer Emiliand Gauthey
in his bridge at Echavannes in Burgundy, later
to be an inspiration for Ledoux's idealisation of
a river surveyors' house [Pl. 6 and pp. 53-57].
Through these regional and rural works, Ledoux
thus prepared himself for a career that encompassed more than the normal programs of a society architect.
Ledoux's two careers, private and public, came
together late in 1771, three weeks after the inaug-

ural fête of Louveciennes, when he was appointed, no doubt through the good offices of Madame
du Barry, but also as a natural extension of his
experience with the administration of the Eaux et
Forêts, "Commissaire des Salines" for Franche-
Comté, Lorraine and the Trois-Évêchés, adjunct
to the Inspecteur des Salines, Perronet himself.[4]
Ledoux thus joined that corps of industrial inspectors established by Colbert and expanded by
Daniel Trudaine in the 1750s, whose role it was
to oversee the quality and processes of manufacture in the royal factories and recommend
construction work where necessary. Another
architect might have treated the position as the
sinecure it was, but Ledoux took his task seriously, and within three years had converted it into
the commission for an entire new salt works in
Franche-Comté, the Saline de Chaux. Supported
by a new patronage circle, including Trudaine
de Montigny, the cultivated *philosophe* and
administrator of commerce, and Haudry de
Soucy, amateur of music and director of salt
works for the Ferme Générale, under whose
management the *salines* were exploited, Ledoux
built, between 1773 and 1778, one of the most
comprehensive model factory villages of the
Ancien Régime.[5]

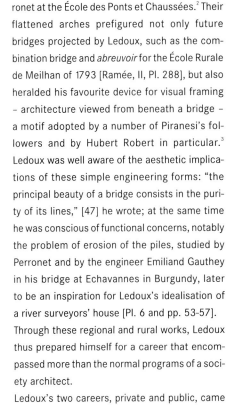

Élévation d'un des Bâtiments d'ouvriers qui forment l'enceinte de la grande Cour.

4. THE ARCHITECTURE OF PRODUCTION

PRODUCTION

Left page:
Saline de Chaux,
director's house.

Above:
Saline de Chaux,
elevation of workers's
building. From:
L'Architecture…,
Ramée edition,
Plate 137.

"It is for the architect to oversee the principle: he can activate the resources of industry, husband its products and avoid costly upkeep; he can augment the treasury by means of the prodigal devices of art." [122]

The salt works of Lorraine and Franche-Comté confided to Ledoux's care in 1771, were, for the most part, ancient foundations: from their Roman and Medieval beginnings, they had continued to produce salt according to a simple process of evaporation from the springs that ran underground in the Jura and lower Alps, slowly crystallising the salt in wide iron pans suspended above wood fires.[1] The result was dried, packed and sold, generally after the 1680s, by the Ferme Générale and subject, except in the regions of production, to the infamous salt-tax, or *gabelle*. The largest of these works at Dieuze, Rosières, Château-Salins and Salins formed self-contained villages in their own right, with their pumps, wells, reservoirs, boiling-pans, furnaces, store-houses, blacksmiths' shops, carpenters' workshops, cooperies, bakeries, wine-presses, administrative offices, apartments for administrators, overseers and workers, chapels, prisons and gatehouses, surrounded by walls and ditches to defend their products against theft and fraud. Ledoux, who must have conducted his tour of inspection before 1773, was unimpressed by their haphazard layout, bad repair and temporary construction

Below:
Saline de Chaux,
plan of the pumps
of the graduation building.
From: *L'Architecture...*,
Plate 8.

Right page, below:
Section of the entry
gate of the Saline and
of the workers' building.
From: *L'Architecture...*,
Plate 36.

that to his eyes "presented a mass of discordant surfaces ... unstable materials, abandoned to chance." [36] Few were working to capacity, many were producing salt of dubious quality, none were susceptible to expansion. Salins, in particular, was forced to waste much of its resources, jettisoning its less concentrated brine for lack of fuel. Already, as the reports of the Ferme Générale had indicated, wood for the furnaces had to be carted from some four leagues distance. Ledoux, utilising previous studies for new *salines* sited nearer to fuel sources, suggested building a factory close to the Forest of Chaux, to which the overspill water of Salins might be piped through an aqueduct; as he wrote, "it was easier to make the water travel than to carry a forest piece by piece." [38] The project was accepted and ordered by Louis XV in April 1773, ratified with the contractor Jean Roux Monclar a year later, and, after Ledoux had produced two plans for the factory, the first stone

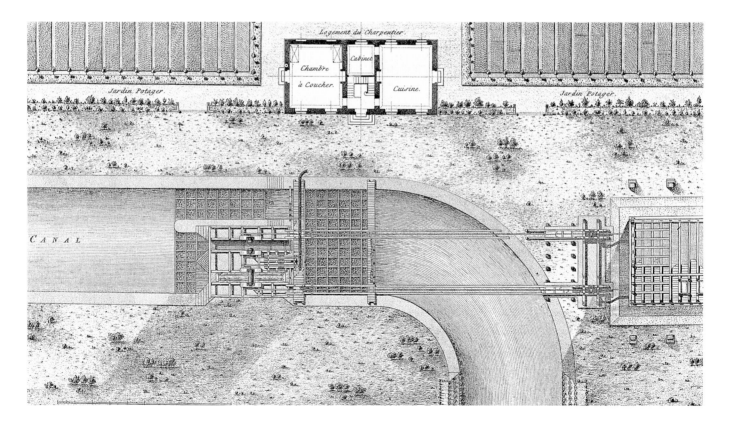

was laid in April 1775.[2] Building work continued for over three years, including the aqueduct from Salins, a double pipeline of drilled fir trunks; the "graduation building" or open frame structure through which the brine was passed in order to partially evaporate it before reaching the stoves; and the pumps and reservoirs.[3]

Ledoux's first project, presented some time before the death of Louis XV in April 1774, was conventional enough: a transformation of the enclosed courtyard plan common to many late seventeenth and eighteenth-century institutions – the Hôpital Saint-Louis in Paris, for example. It distributed the functions of living and working

Above:
Perspective view of the entry gate of the Saline. From: *L'Architecture...*, Plate 35.

Pages 42-43:
Saline de Chaux, the columns of the entrance seen from the grotto.

Pages 44-45:
Saline de Chaux, perspective view of the graduation building. From: *L'Architecture...*, Plate 9.

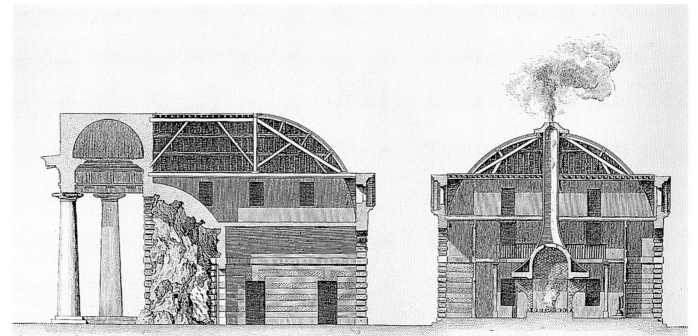

Coupe de la Porte d'entrée de la Saline de Chaux, sur la Ligne. AB.

Coupe sur la Ligne AB. du Batiment des Berniers.

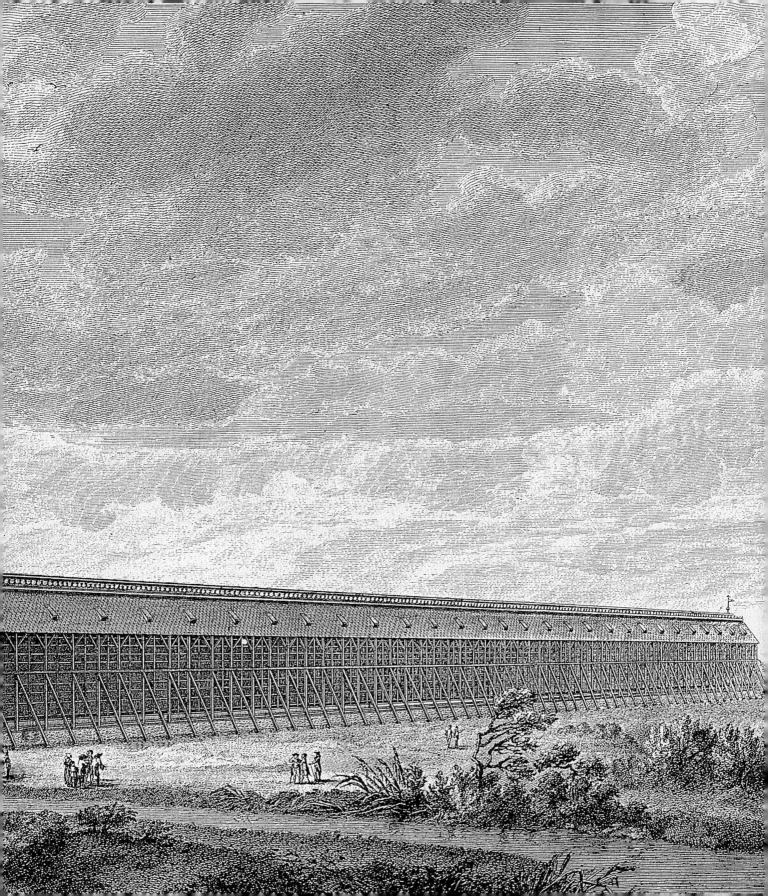

Right page:
Saline de Chaux,
general plan.
From: *L'Architecture...*,
Plate 16.

Right page below:
First plan of the Saline
de Chaux, not realised.
From: *L'Architecture...*,
Plate 12.

in a continuous structure around the square central courtyard, used to stack the wood-fuel. At the corners and at the centre of each side, square two-story pavilions contained the major functions: the gatehouse, chapel and bakery to the front, the workshops of the blacksmiths and coopers to the sides, and the factory to the rear. In between, to either side, were apartments for the workers, arranged around central fireplaces, and across the front elevation stretched the administrative offices. The entire factory, surrounded by kitchen gardens for the workers to supplement their salaries, and a high wall seemed to mirror the almost monastic regime of the traditional Colbertian factory. Where Ledoux attempted innovation, however, was in the rigorous subjection of the heterogeneous functions to an overall geometry; in the provision of diagonal covered galleries across the courtyard as a means, Ledoux stated, of "accelerating all the services;" and in the architectural expression of the factory as a whole.

In this last concern, the invention of an aesthetic proper to manufacturing, Ledoux encountered incredulity, from the Ferme and its agents. A factory, even in the inclusive theory of Blondel, was low on the scale in the hierarchy of building-types; its ordering, Blondel stated, should be simple without presenting too military an aspect.[4] Columns and architectural motifs, if they were present at all, should be confined to the main entrance, as, for example, in Blondel's design for the Royal Tobacco Factory at Morlaix. Ledoux, not content with so reductive a means of characterisation, attempted to adapt the "rusticated" motifs of Palladio and Serlio together with the dramatic simplicity of the primitive Doric, to constitute what for him represented an "architecture of production." Four giant rusticated columns defended the entry; twenty-four others supported three covered porches to the rear; the coopery and smithy each had Serlian doorways; the covered galleries, like the stoas of Greece so lyrically described by David Le Roy, rested on 140 baseless Doric columns. Other columns encircled the chapel and decorated the entrance to the bakery. In this display of embellishment, Ledoux was directly and self-consciously countering the prevailing code of luxury and *convenance*; Ledoux recalled that Louis XV was offended by this overturning of the representational rules of the First Estate, asking "Why so many columns – they are only suitable for temples and royal palaces?" In justification Ledoux explained, "the columns used in these buildings cannot be found in churches, royal palaces, or individual houses." [40] Similarly offensive to the established codes was Ledoux's cavalier placement of the chapel as if equal in value to the bakery, and banished to a corner of the plan.

But it does not seem that this first project was rejected on these grounds alone: Ledoux speaks of changes forced by the programme, more precisely defined in the contract of 1774, and by knowledge of the site, not selected finally until the end of that year.[5] Ledoux himself began to re-think his plan, with respect both to the functioning of the works and its proper characterisation. This was evidently tied to a more general discussion of the nature of institutional form that erupted in the early 1770s in the debate over the replacement of the old Hôtel-Dieu on the Ile de la Cité, damaged by fire in 1772, a debate in which Ledoux was directly involved.[6] When, in retrospect, Ledoux noted that his first project for the Saline had been too centralised, unhygienic and a fire hazard, he was unmistakably referring to the criteria proposed by doctors and administrators for the design of hospitals and other public buildings in the 1770s.[7] He wrote: "The architect felt that everything should be isolated; that the communal and individual dwellings, the furnaces should be sheltered from proximity, that is always to be feared when hemmed in by the multitude. He felt that he should compose with the winds that ensure health." [67] Such concerns had become a commonplace after 1772, the basis for schemes for hospitals drawn up by the doctor Antoine Petit (1774), and the architect Bernard Poyet much later. Petit, who proposed a circular plan with ward-blocks distributed like the spokes of a wheel around a central, conical pavilion containing kitchens and chapel, had

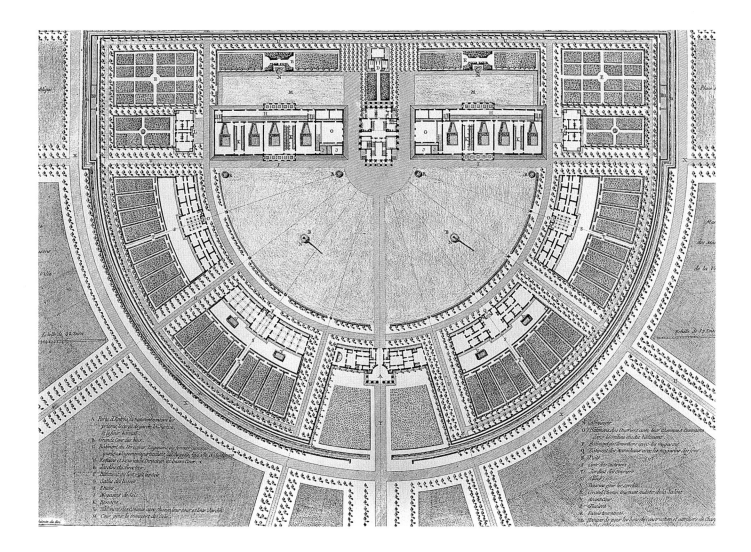

similarly argued against a square plan, "la forme quarrée," as uneconomic for service and encouraging of stagnant water.[8]

In this context the final semi-circular plan for the Saline, unifying a number of separate pavilions around its periphery and across its rear diameter, may be interpreted on one level as a gesture towards this discourse of institutional form. What had before been a single factory building, now became broken up into the constituent parts of a factory town planned, like Vitruvius's city of the winds, to take advantage of breezes from different quarters, at once dispersing smoke and fumes from the evaporation process and promoting the health of the inhabitants. "The first laws are those of nature," wrote Ledoux, "those that ensure the health of the inhabitants and determine their well-being on a preferred site. These first laws command the winds." [69]

On another level, however, Ledoux's intentions were entirely aesthetic: the semi-circle was an effective device for visually linking the different structures, each properly characterised according to function and role, that in the open picturesque landscape of the Loue valley might resemble the pavilions of an English landscape

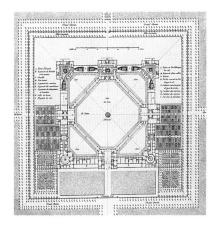

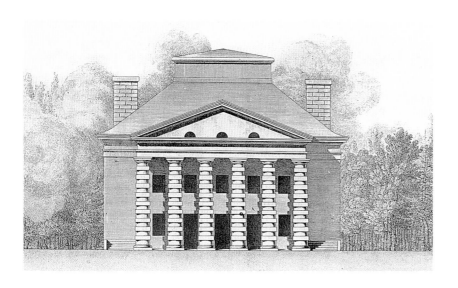

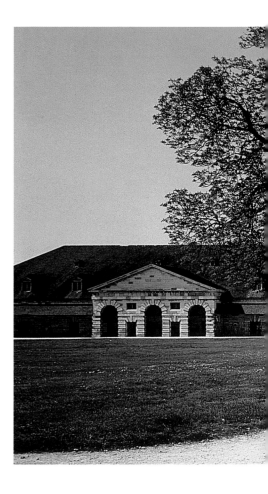

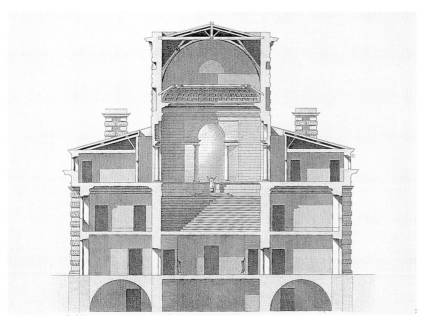

Above left:
Saline de Chaux,
elevation of the
director's house.
From: *L'Architecture*...,
Plate 71.

Below left:
Section of the
director's house.
From: *L'Architecture*...,
Plate 64.

Above right and right page:
Saline de Chaux,
"Avenue of power".
Panoramic view of
the director's house
and the factory sheds.

garden. Further, the specific form and proportions of the semi-circle indicate Ledoux's overall symbolic aim: the Saline is, literally, to be read as a theatre, as it follows the outlines of the antique amphitheatre, described by Vitruvius and illustrated by Perrault.[9] Here Ledoux was again responding to a contemporary debate: the question of the proper form for public theatres, opened by Soufflot, Cochin and Dumont after 1750, and sustained by de Wailly's and Peyre's plans for the Théâtre-Français.[10] As type and metaphor, the theatrical plan controlled and gave substance to Ledoux's complex mixture of social and political idealism at Chaux, balanced between a pre-panoptical symbolism of surveillance and a proto-Rouseauesque model of community. It also unified his decorative programme and supplied an appropriate theatrical allegory

for the production of salt. The semi-circle finally was, as demonstrated by the Place Royale at Dijon, the seventeenth-century projects for Places Royales in Paris, and the newly published projects for squares to exhibit statues of Louis XV, a fundamentally royal form, at once crown and center of power.

As designed and built, and as, albeit severely restored, it stands today, the Saline comprises ten major buildings, together with their outhouses and stables, ranged along the perimeter of a semi-circle over four hundred meters in diameter. The five pavilions that curve around the hemi-cycle are roughly similar in plan and three-dimensional massing, each with a central double-height space roofed beneath a pyramidal mansard, flanked by single-story wings. Each was modified on the interior to accommodate its

different functions. Thus the main gatehouse is entered through a portico of six baseless Doric columns topped by a deep architrave, evidently imitating David Le Roy's illustration of the Propylaea of the Acropolis.[11] Behind these columns, the doorway is set into an imitation stone grotto, decorated with carved urns spouting stylised pendants of crystallised salt water.[12] The wings of the gatehouse contained a fresh-water reservoir, bakery, apartments for the guards and porters, a room for the visiting judge and a prison cell for temporary detention. The coopery and the carpenters' shops to the west, and the smithy and forge to the east flank this monumental gatehouse. Apartments for the craftsmen were installed on the second story of the central entrance space in each case, and a gallery looked down to the communal hearth below. Completing the amphitheatre are the buildings that housed the salt workers themselves, serving the western and eastern factory sheds respectively. Each of these buildings had twelve apartments, six to a wing, arranged along a corridor that led to the double-height communal space.

To the rear of the plan are the administrative and manufacturing buildings. At the centre, directly opposite the gatehouse, is the director's building, fronted by a portico of giant rusticated columns surmounted by a pediment, with a steep pyramidal roof crowning the central volume of the building behind. Inside was the chapel, reached by a continuous flight of stairs that mounted diagonally toward the back of the building, to the altar lit from the rear. The apartments and offices of the director and the agents of the Ferme surrounded the chapel on two levels. The two factory sheds, each containing boiling-pans, reservoirs and drying racks, and fronted by neo-Palladian porches in rusticated stone, stand on either side of the director's building. At each corner of the Saline are detached pavilions that housed the clerks and overseers. Behind the director's building is a coach house and stables, and behind each workers' building a small stone shed for garden tools and kitchen gardens for cultivating food. A high wall surrounds the entire factory. A dry ditch and a perimeter "boulevard" completed the protective *enceinte*.

The architecture of this ensemble is unabashedly theatrical, a dramatic combination of abstract three-dimensional geometries that define the volumes of each pavilion, and architectural motifs that stand out against the smooth cut stone and boldly pitched tile-roofs. These motifs – the entrance porches, rusticated, double-height serliana, carved urns and water spouts in bas-relief – are like so many set-pieces attached to the primary forms of *besoin*, an almost direct fulfilment of d'Alembert's definition of architecture. For Ledoux this architecture held a double symbolism: on the one hand, the ever-present power of the director and his associates, overseeing production as agents of royal authority; on the other, a carefully structured community of artisans and workers, designed to encourage sociability and moralisation. These two levels of signification are directly incorporated into the architectural organization. The first, that of surveillance, is represented by an "axis of power" that leads from the entrance to the director's building, marked along the route by a series of motifs that establish an allegory of natural, industrial and administrative surveillance: from the

Élévation des remises du Directeur.

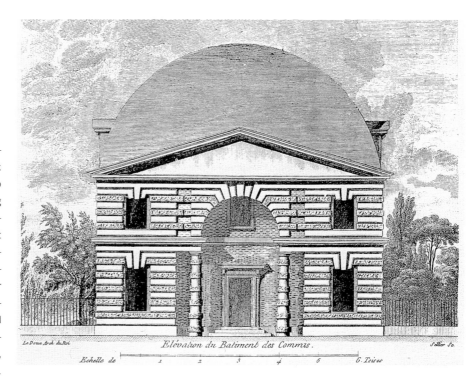

Elévation du Batiment des Commis.

portico of the gatehouse, with its columns guarding the natural sources of production, the mock grotto emulating the salt springs, to the portico of the director's house, and thence ascending stage by stage to the illuminated focus of spiritual power, these motifs stage a narrative that moves from nature through production to worship. Countering this axis, the curve of the semi-circle, re-assembles the communality of worker life, bonded in smaller units around their central hearths and grouped as a collective around the overall "foyer" of benefits, the centre of direction. "Placed at the centre of the lines of sight, nothing escapes his surveillance," Ledoux wrote. Describing his plan for the Saline Ledoux was insistent on what he considered the principal virtue of the semi-circle – its ability to facilitate what he called surveillance. Concerns of oversight and economy had been present in the first project: "the clerk overseer oversees everything; placed at the centre of the converging lines of sight," Ledoux had written, "he can comprise in a single glance the details under his supervision."[67] The literal image of these lines of sight, however, had only become visible in the semi-circle. Unobstructed vision, facilitated by the architect, was Ledoux's answer to the complicated system of administrative control, of work and of worker behaviour, demanded by the codes of the Salines Royales: "The eye easily oversees the shortest line; the work crosses it with a rapid

step; the burden of the passage is lightened by the anticipation of a swift return. Everything obeys the scheme that perfects the law of movement." [77] Such an obvious correlation between geometry, movement and visual control has seemed to some commentators a confirmation of Ledoux's panopticism, an anticipation of a form of oversight perfected by Jeremy Bentham for his project of a Panopticon in the 1790s. Michel Foucault, notably, has seen in this plan a sort of "machine à surveiller," a "perfect disciplinary apparatus," an intimation of Bentham's system: "a central point would be at the same time a source of light illuminating everything and a place of convergence for everything that should be seen: the perfect eye from which nothing escapes and a centre towards which all gazes are turned."[13]

But Ledoux's own discourse, while supporting this interpretation to the extent that for example the director's house is called, in the *Prospectus* to *L'Architecture*, a "Temple de surveillance," nevertheless is more mediated on the architectural level than Bentham's later machine-like model. He seems more intent to register the symbolic presence of power than the actual functionalisation of visual oversight. Thus hedges sheltered the workers' buildings from immediate scrutiny and the director's house itself is indeed more a temple than an overseer's cage. Again the theatrical allusion betrays the complexity of Ledoux's idealising politics, as exemplified in the celebrated engraving of the "coup d'oeil" of the Theatre of Besançon [Plate 113]: there, an empty auditorium is seen reflected in the pupil of an eye; the eye also reflects a beam of light that extends from the rear of the *salle* to the stage, as if illuminating the actor (or director?) to whom the eye belongs; but this beam is extended once more from the eye itself to project beyond the pupil as if to light the observer of the image, in the position of the spectator. This doubled reflection constructs reciprocity between audience and actor, society and its law-givers, workers and director, that also seems to be the "play" enacted in the Saline. Here too, the section of the director's house, resembling the steps of an auditorium, but, so to speak, at the centre of the stage itself, turning the assembled workers in the chapel into an audience before their own "auditorium," replicates in three-dimensions what Ledoux implies for Besançon.

Such a symbolisation of power is given further force by the resemblance of the director's building to a masonic temple, pronounced in the first project, with its chapel echoing the geometries of a masonic lodge, and its massing resembling restorations of Solomon's Temple from Perrault to Fischer von Erlach. The second project is less "primitive," yet also resembles many contemporary figurations of the "temple" in masonic floor-drawings and iconographies.[14] The "initiatory" effect of the architecture was unmistakably similar to that of many theatrical performances, which, for the Parisian audiences of the 1770s during the first period of masonic fashion, held overtones of the lodge. Certainly Ledoux's mise-en-scène paralleled that of the first performance of Gluck's *Orphée et Eurydice* in Paris on the 2nd August 1774, with its six acts, staged like a masonic initiation, that moved from the laurel and cypress groves where Eurydice was buried, past the Furies, into the abyss of Lethe, through a cave of terrifying darkness, across the River Cocytus, finally to emerge in a delightful garden facing a magnificent "Temple of Love."[15] Ledoux, a supporter of the newly fashionable music of Christoph Gluck against the admirers of Niccolò Piccinni, was later to describe his visit to the Salines of Salins in almost the same terms, speaking of his descent into the underground springs beneath the factory as if it had been a visit to the realm of Lethe guided by the boatman Charon.

The symbolism of the Egyptian underworld, so popular in lodges and theatre alike following the publication of the Abbé Terasson's novel *Séthos*, was sustained in the dramatic back-drop of the "theatre of production" where Ledoux adopted the pyramid as the basic form for director's building and factory buildings that all, with their steeply pitched roofs, implied completion according to the geometries of the Great Pyramid. The truncated pyramid of the director's building imaged that of masonic symbolism, with the triangle of the "all-seeing eye" taken up by the top-light of the chapel. The section of the factory furnaces took the allegory further, and emulated what for Ledoux and many of his contemporaries was thought to be the "origin" of the form of Egyptian mausoleums: the idea of a tapering flame burning on the pyres of the Pharaohs was transferred to the smoking fires of the factory; in cross-section Ledoux reinforces this analogy by extending the shadow of the roofs to the ground to form a perfect pyramid. Finally, the factory sheds are entered through rusticated, three-arched porches that seem to be directly taken from the neo-Palladian entries inscribed by Fischer von Erlach to his imaginary reconstructions of the pyramids. After the Revolution, Ledoux, no doubt wishing to take his distance from the pyramidal crematoria designed by Pierre Giraud for the victims of the Terror, distinguished between his own "productive sublime," and that of political immolation: "one must distinguish the saline vapours that envelop the roofs of the factory from the putrid smoke exhaled from the altars where the victims burn." [119]

"Five elevations each fifty-four meters long, describe a vast circle, with the space in between planted with useful trees": in this way, countering the forbidding motifs of his Sarastrian elegy, Ledoux eulogised the communitarian spaces of familial life. At the centre of each workers' building was an "hôtel de réunion," or family room, to either side of which were six four-bed apartments: "each room is occupied by a family; a gallery leads to a common hearth. This hearth

Below:
Saline de Chaux,
perspective view
of the director's house.
From: *L'Architecture...*,
Plate 60.

Pages 54-55:
Saline de Chaux,
director's house,
view at night.

Pages 56-57:
Entrance grotto
of the Saline,
view at night.

provides all the means to prepare and watch over the foodstuffs; the clay in which they boil covers a hundred stoves sustained by a continuous flame." Around this fireside Ledoux imagined lazy evenings of a Rousseauesque happiness, confirmed by a domed section that, he noted, "gives a general idea of the mutual reconciliation that recalls man to the social order, taken from nature."[l09] Like Rousseau who posited that "the first developments of the heart were the effect of a new situation that brought together in a single dwelling husbands and wives, fathers and children,"[16] Ledoux believed in the civilising effect of his spaces: "it is in these charming places that everything is enjoyment; it is there that love has set down its fidelity, there it is that man is still arrayed in his innocence." [110] The workers' buildings would, he hoped, become "preferred places," wherein life would be lived according to "natural laws." [111] And if the ill-paid and over-worked *salineur* had little in the way of property, at least he would, like a spectator at a play, be "surrounded by the sweetest illusions," during the hours of rest. More importantly for the smooth running of the factory, he would equally be "sheltered from all costly distractions and Bacchic deliria that could disturb Hymen, and tempt or surprise laziness." Inside, "he finds his pleasures, the consolation for his labours, and the solution for all his needs;" outside, "if he leaves these delightful retreats, it is to cultivate a productive field that

fills the intervals of work and amuses his leisure." [111] Leisure time would thus be functionalised on behalf of production; the workers would remain "attached to the soil," while their food would be supplied at no cost to the employer. In his model of a happy manufacturing community, Ledoux shares the views of the author of the article "Manufacture" in the *Encyclopédie* who argued against the over-constrained environment of the centralised factory on behalf of a more dispersed industry, where the worker had more liberty and therefore more "equality" with the master.[17]

Ledoux was also, as subsequent historians have pointed out, anticipating the re-construction of the "feudal" relations of the seigniorial village in the factory towns of the nineteenth century, from Robert Owen at New Lanark to Titus Salt at Saltaire. For this elaborate and idealised setting sheltered a factory community that was, for all intents and purposes, self-sustaining. Some two hundred workers, living together with their families, supplied by a common bakery, with vegetable gardens and orchards, were, within the twelve-foot-high wall, managed by a strict hier-

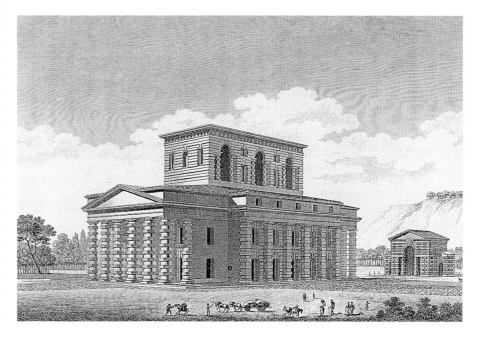

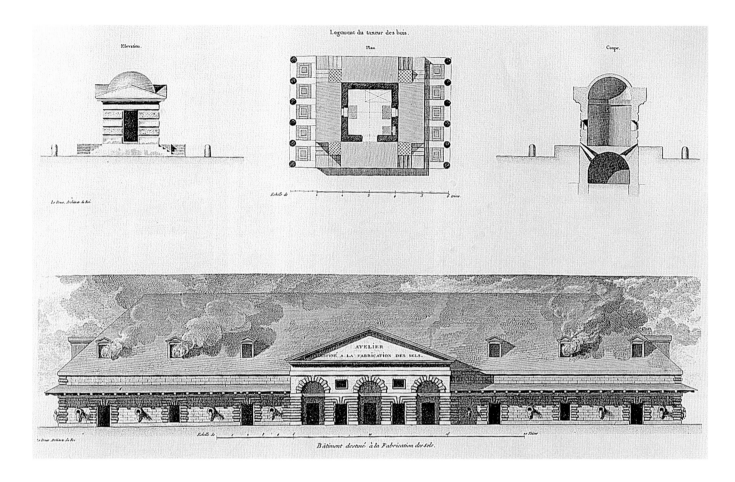

archy of officials, from the director, his inspectors and clerks to the porters, guards and overseers. Regulations ordered the day of each inhabitant, from morning prayers to curfew; work procedures were rigidly controlled, divided according to traditional tasks and metiers, timed according to the calculation of scientists. The use of fuel and other materials was carefully watched, outgoing and incoming products were counted, weighed and measured. A virtual fortress from the outside – even the agents of the Ferme required a written pass to enter – it was a miniature kingdom inside, over which the director and his officials ruled, as the historian Pierre Boyé put it, like a small band of tyrants.

This ramified administration began at the gatehouse, which housed the offices of the porters, responsible for controlling movements in and out of the factory, enforcing the workers' timetable and registering goods and services. "It is in this centre of enlightenment," wrote Ledoux, "that the indefatigable eye of vigilance follows the respective interests of the hours and of those who employ them," [109] closely paraphrasing the orders drawn up by Haudry for the gatekeepers in 1775. [18] The centre of surveillance was the director's building, within which the different functions were organised according to social and legal rank. The basement accommodated the "employés subalternes," the wine cellar, wood stores; on the ground floor was the accounting office, a bank, a council chamber for the Fermiers, and a courtroom for the chief visiting judge – "the halls where Themis renders justice." [131] Also on this floor were a kitchen, a doctor's office with storage for medicinal herbs, and a laboratory for the resident chemist. On the first floor were the private apartments of the director and high officials, a dining room, a salon, bedrooms and offices. The central activity of the Saline was, of course, the fabrication of the salt, its evaporation, drying and packing in the two factory sheds or *bernes* to either side of the director's building, joined together by a covered passage that ran beneath the stairs of the chapel. In these huge barns, the brigades of workers set up the boiling pans or *poêles*, made out of hundreds of riveted iron plates, and suspended above the furnaces by means of rods tied into the thick wooden beams that spanned the pans. Other workers stoked the fires, prepared the pans for evaporation by caulking, and gradually let in the brine, maintaining a constant heat and periodically skimming the surface to remove the impurities.

Others, again, after the continuous forty-eight hours of slow boiling had crystallised the salt, raked off the wet salt onto the drying racks. Finally, in the packing rooms, or *salles des bosses*, the salt was moulded into flat cakes or packed into panniers for export.

In planning these *bernes* Ledoux followed the traditional layout of the *poêles*, arranging them in pairs on either side of their drying racks and in front of the long stove for the drying of the cakes; but he improved considerably on the distribution of heat from the furnaces and thereby the conservation of fuel. He separated each stove from the next by insulating walls built out of hollow bricks, and connected the stoves to a *modérateur* or chimney, to warm the drying rooms above. He also, but to no avail, argued for the increasing utilisation of coal over wood, a practice that was not adopted until well into the nineteenth century. Finally, he allowed for better oversight of the work by providing an upper-level gallery looking down on the *poêles*, connected to the apartment of the Inspecteur des Poêles, who resided in the pediment over the porch.

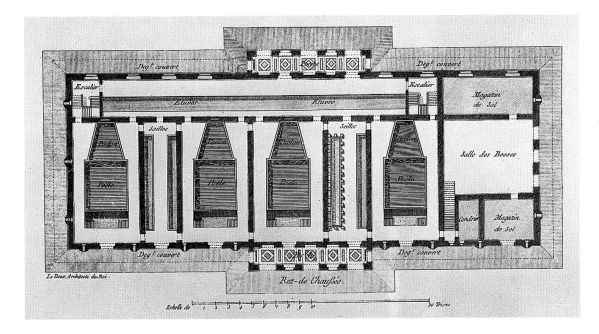

Left page:
Saline de Chaux,
elevation of the
salt production building.
From: *L'Architecture…*,
Ramée edition,
Plate 132.

Detailed plan
of the salt production
building.
From: *L'Architecture…*,
Plate 41.

Following double page:
Back facade
of the western
factory sheds.

Following double page:
Saline de Chaux,
perspective view
of the ironworks.
From: *L'Architecture…*,
Plate 125.

Facade in front
of the factory
sheds.

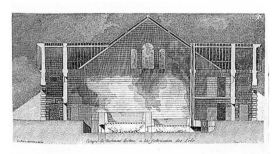

Section of the
furnaces of the Saline.
From: *L'Architecture…*,
Plates 47 and 48.

Despite Ledoux's idealisation of the factory shed as a sublime evocation of production, its windows belching thick "Egyptian" smoke as if from some primitive funereal pyre, working conditions were virtually insufferable. The thick steam, mingled with the acidic vapours and smoke from the furnaces, together with the intense heat, made breathing difficult; ventilation was non-existent. The workers, afflicted by chronic bronchial and mucous diseases, often partially disabled from accidents – loss of limbs from falling into the boiling brine or of eyes due to the flames was common – worked in twelve-hour shifts, day and night, for the pitiful sum of six *sous* per day.[19] Sustaining this continuous production was a wide-flung external economy of wood, iron and metiers in the forest of Chaux, supported by a work force of woodcutters, charcoal-burners, coopers, carters, sawyers and ironworkers. These external workers, often difficult to manage and resistant to authority, were, like the internal workers of the Saline, subject to the surveillance of forest guards, officers of the crown and of the *salines*.[20] Ledoux was to make them the object of a similar architectural paternalism after the 1780s in his projects for dwellings and workshops for the artisans of the forest, that, however "utopian" all had their roots in this veritable "civilisation of wood" in Franche-Comté.

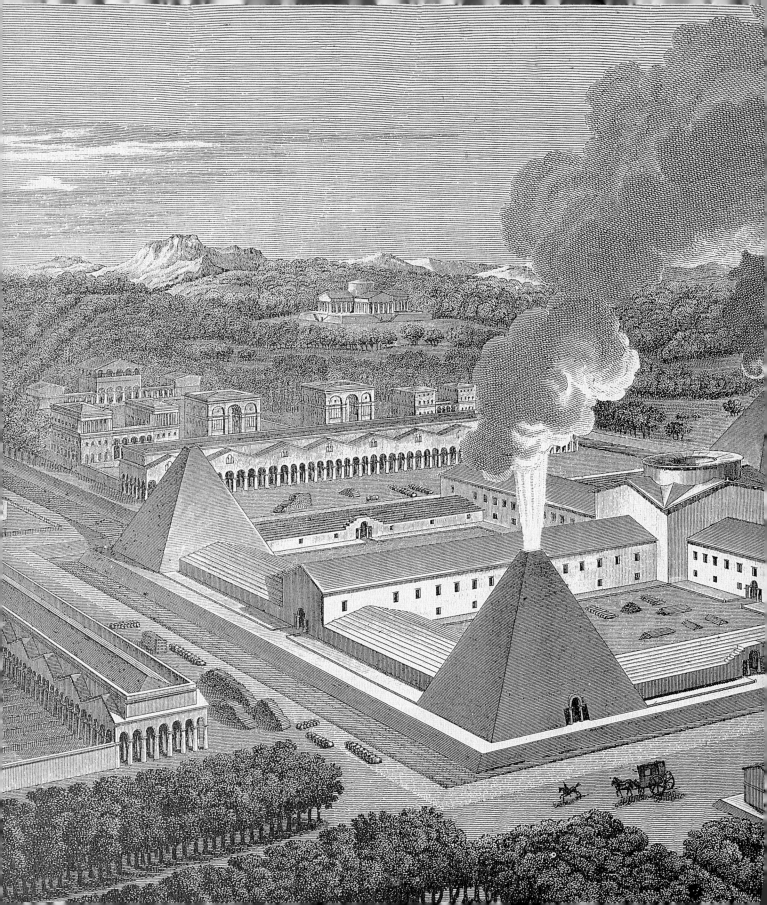

5. LANGUAGES OF CHARACTER

"The character of monuments, like their nature, serves for the propagation and purification of mores. There are erected theatres in the progressive form that levels humanity; here are triumphal arches that deify it." [3]

Between 1775 and 1789, from the laying of the foundation stone of the Saline to the Revolution, Ledoux, despite numerous setbacks real and imagined, developed one of the most brilliant and successful architectural practices of the last years of the Ancien Régime. Boullée, older, may have gained more academic rewards, but after 1780 he built little; Gondouin was associated with the École de Chirurgie, Charles de Wailly with the Théâtre-Français, Antoine with the Hôtel des Monnaies, and Rousseau with the Hôtel de Salm. Brongniart and Bélanger forged rich private practices for fashionable patrons. Ledoux, however, while continuing to expand his patronage for private hotels and housing developments in Paris, found his real interest in public commissions. Patronised until the end by the Ferme Générale, he built a salt warehouse at Compiègne, began the construction of a huge new headquarters for the offices of the Ferme in Paris, and supervised the erection of the sixty or more tollgates accompanying the wall of the Ferme Générale between 1784 and 1789. He turned the support of Trudaine de Montigny to good account in Besançon, where he received the commission for

Right page:
The columns
in front of the grotto
at the entry of the
Saline de Chaux.

Below:
Columns of the
director's house.

a new theatre from de Lacoré, Intendant of Franche-Comté, and in Aix-en-Provence, where, introduced to Gallois de La Tour, Intendant and First President of the Parliament of Aix, he designed successive projects for a new Palace of Justice and Prisons. Called to Hesse-Cassel by Frederick II, he worked on a project for a triumphal arch, redesigned the royal library and museum, and conceived grandiose plans for a new palace. Following up every lead with enthusiasm, he submitted projects for a discount bank to Turgot and Calonne, plans for a new theatre for Marseille, a Hôtel de Ville for Neuchâtel, and for markets in the rue Saint-Germain, Paris.

During these years, Ledoux also found his place as a member of Parisian society. Recovering from the loss of patronage suffered by the disgrace of du Barry and the fall of Turgot, he used his position as member of the Academy and favoured architect of the Ferme to good effect. His connections with the Marquis de Montesquiou reinforced his literary friendships, notably to the Abbé Delille, whose translations of Virgil (*Les Georgiques*) and prose poems (*Les Jardins*) influenced

his vision of landscape and rural reform: Hubert Robert, Watelet, de Wailly, and Brongniart, completed the artistic circle. This society was as linked by common interests in the theatre and the opera, as it was by more self-conscious sociability in the freemasonic lodges. Ledoux, whose name, unlike those of over a hundred other Parisian architects from 1774 to 1789, does not appear on the lists of the Grand Orient lodges, was, on the testimony of the English writer William Beckford, certainly affiliated to a lodge of a more unorthodox kind in the mid-1780s. His architectural symbolism during this epoch, his plans and utopian discourse after the Revolution both testify to a strong freemasonic influence. Ledoux, who, as Cellerier attested, "loved society in general, but preferred that of artists and women," was just at ease in the salons of rich hostesses, like that of Madame Thélusson, widow of the Swiss banker to whom he had been introduced by Haudry of the Ferme Générale, as he was in the somewhat military, exclusively male, ambiance of the lodges.

Sharing in the sociability of this milieu, Ledoux also found support for an architecture with pretensions to social as well as to aesthetic reform. What in the 1750s had been the polemical preserve of a few *philosophes* and enlightened architects, had, by the late 1770s, become a commonplace of administrative concern: the demand for an embellished city.[1] By this was meant not

Saline de Chaux,
roofing of the
guards' building and
the cooper's building

Right page:
The columns
of the director's house.

Below:
Detail of the grotto
at the entry of the Saline.

simply the planting of trees, the decoration of facades and the provision of fountains, but a more or less systematic reconstruction of the urban fabric, including the planning of networks for the circulation of traffic, water and air; provisions for sanitation, fire-prevention, street lighting; the re-locating of "unhealthy" institutions such as cemeteries, hospitals, abattoirs; the redesign of institutions devoted to social welfare – hospices, prisons, schools; the opening up of the old city for trade and commerce. Despite local disagreements, the overall form of the new city was generally agreed: Sébastien Mercier described it in his utopian novel *L'an 2240*, Pierre Patte contributed technical reports and illustrated it in plan in his composite assemblage of competition entries for a Place Louis XV in Paris, the Abbé Lubersac celebrated its monumental aesthetics in pompous eulogies.[2] Visually, the city would take on the aspect of a hunting park, with its pathways turned into boulevards and its crossings into public squares. The important monuments of display, pleasure and public utility would be scattered throughout, set in open spaces of their own, properly characterised by their architectural orders, emblematic decoration and form.

Interpreted in this theoretical context, Ledoux's designs for public institutions before the Revolution can be seen to stand apart from the accepted solutions on at least two levels: on the one hand he showed himself unwilling to follow the reductive and diagrammatic "functionalism" of the doctors and lawyers, while on the other, understanding the limits of a literal neo-classical historicism in the representation of new or radically re-defined programmes, he sought to define a genre and a style detached somewhat from precise cultural reference. To this end he founded his conception of character on the double play of three-dimensional distribution – the constitutive form of the type – and abstract allusion – a kind of generic classicism that, while precise enough in identifying its sources, nevertheless partook of the overall language of geometricised form. Thus, for Ledoux, the unifying force of stereotomy allowed a form, such as the cube subdivided into nine squares in each dimension, to become a figure – an unambiguous reference to Palladio – without any perceptible division or differentiation. The same mechanism that permitted the alternating cubes and cylinders of a rusticated column to stand at once for "Serlio" and for a microcosm of the geometrical form of the building as a whole also operated from the largest scale to the smallest.

Within the parameters of such abstraction, Ledoux was, as the Saline de Chaux had demonstrated, entirely open to the use of historical precedent. But his historicism was far from revivalist in the sense established by younger antiquarian enthusiasts such as Quatremère de Quincy or Séroux d'Agincourt with their sense of anachronism and relative value.[3] From Blondel's lectures, and more especially from David Le Roy's publications of Greek monuments, Ledoux derived a vision of antiquity entirely disposable for contemporary use. Le Roy's presentation of Athens as both ruined and "restored", fragmented and typical, gave Ledoux his structural and semantic models. Ruins, as Diderot had noted, showed the past as so many fragments, analytically broken down into its component parts, the "signs" of ancient culture. Perfected

types, on the other hand, that represented the crystallisation of social institutions in simple and closed forms embodied principles of distribution. The former acted, like a hieroglyph or pictogram, to identify and signify; the latter composed and constituted diverse functions in typical patterns. Brought together, united by the intersecting play of geometry, figurative devices, and formal structures, they emerged as monuments that were at once historically allusive and generically typical: an architecture that, in Ledoux's terms, "spoke" to the sensations through the eyes. This last appeal to the sensations, one common enough in the latter eighteenth century following Diderot, Condillac and Helvétius, was accomplished for Ledoux through the category of the sublime, newly re-defined by Edmund Burke. No longer a traditional commonplace of rhetorical style, as understood by Boileau through Longinus, and repeated as a specific genre by Blondel in treating of buildings requiring an "exalted" style or a "terrible" effect, the sublime became in the work and writing of Ledoux an all-embracing quality of public architecture, a guarantee of the emotional and intellectual effect of monuments as they not only represented their type and genre, but expressed appropriate ideas and evoked powerful sensations in their viewers. In the Saline de Chaux, Ledoux had already explored the roster of sublime effects described by Burke in his *Philosophical Enquiry into the Origin of Our Ideas of the Sublime and Beautiful* (1757-1759; translated into French, 1765). Burke's insistence on the "origin" of the sublime in terror, and his call for the production "of the strongest emotion which the mind is capable of feeling" established the sublime as by far the most interesting of aesthetic criteria, relegating the "beautiful" to a static, classical notion all too easily achieved by symmetry and balance. Using architecture as his central example of the "artificial sublime": Burke had delineated what for Ledoux and Boullée were to become the ingredients of their "public sublime": darkness, confusion, uncertainty, producing religious terror in the temples of the ancients and the forests of the Druids; vacuity, absence of light, solitude and silence leading to impressions of infinity and thereby of unlimited power; vastness of height, length and breadth, magnificence and splendour, all properties that would "raise the mind of the observer, seize it and astonish it." Burke helpfully suggested recipes for architects: the "artificial infinite" was to be produced by a combination of succession and uniformity in the parts of a building – as in a rotunda, where no boundary interferes with the turning of the eye, or in a row of similar columns, devoid of interruption or break. Brilliant contrasts of light and shade, the play of absolute darkness and total illumination, enormous scale and rude gigantism (such as at Stonehenge), sombre colours, and the use of magnificent materials, completed the somewhat dramatic repertory outlined by Burke.[4]

Ledoux exploited all these effects, from the pyramidal massing of the Saline to its semi-circular plan, where nothing would stop the sweep of vision, effects which in Burke had also been related to the fundamental effects of natural scenery. Emphasising the necessity for a primitive simplicity, later to be reiterated by Kant, Ledoux produced a genre that encompassed all the building tasks of the public realm. Eschewing the Piranesian panoply of emblems and attributes, popular in Delafosse and Neufforge, he reduced his style to essentials – primary geometric solids, bare walls relieved only by the contrast of a few dramatically carved bas-reliefs, square or round, unfluted, Doric columns and pilasters without bases, geometrical rustication – all combined to provide almost scenic effects for the "voyageur" who passed in front of these facades in combinatorial movement, or who moved himself through volumes lit from above, ascending long ranges of stairs as if climbing some sacred mountainside. "Do you wish to produce effects independent of these conventional motifs that shrink the vastness of nature?" wrote Ledoux, "you will see that the only way permitted by the economy of art will lead you towards the sublime. Establish beautiful masses, abandon those affectations too much cherished by fearful custom, those multiplied mouldings, those

children born of blind fathers who have never savoured the pleasures of light." [204] Reconstruing in this way the demand for character, enunciated by Blondel in formulaic terms, and by Boffrand in relation to poetic conventions, Ledoux refused both the paradox of d'Alembert and the hierarchy of genres dear to Blondel; all public buildings, including the smallest dwelling constructed by the government, were susceptible to the same power of effect; all should be invested with a touch of the sublime, from the artisan's cottage to the palace of justice. What for later philosophers including Hegel would become a category of expression best returned to its religious origins, a sublime already overcome by history, was readily adopted by Ledoux as the proper language of an architect whose self-avowed role as the earthly delegate of the Creator required a manner of expression suitable to the sacralisation of new secular subjects.

6. GALLO-ROMAN ANTIQUITY

"My imagination wanders. It is transported to those sumptuous monuments that transmit to posterity the power of the emperors, the grandeur of Charlemagne. Nothing can contain the torrent that carries it; it penetrates those vaults that distribute abundance … those caverns that conceal the treasures of the Caesars [the grottoes of Auxelles]. It expands with the trace of their conquests, with those arches that recall their victories [the arch of Besançon]." [73]

If Ledoux exploited all the techniques of the spatial sublime outlined by Burke and later systematised by Kant, he did not neglect the evocation of the temporal or historical sublime that was to become the leitmotif of Romantic historicism. But unlike his contemporaries whose historical reference was grounded in Rome and the circle of Piranesians, Ledoux identified another foundational antiquity: that of the Gallo-Roman epoch and its remains in Franche-Comté and Provence. From the early 1770s, his widening travels in France had confirmed his early allegiance to the mythic origins of the French nation, that had left its heraldic and monumental traces in remains from the salt works of Salins, (Roman in foundation), the Porte Noire of Besançon, with its allegorical bas-reliefs, to the complete repertory of Roman types in the Midi, at Nîmes, Arles, Orange, Marseille and Aix-en-Provence.[1] His experience

Left page:
Column in the forest
of Chaux, an instance
of Ledoux's language
in a different
environment.

Above:
One of Ledoux's
references:
the arch of triumph
and the mausoleum
of Julians,
Saint-Rémy-
de-Provence.

Detail of the
Barrière d'Enfer

Right page:
The Porte Noire
in Besançon.
The part of the
drawing that is below
the arch corresponds
to the latest additions
which were
destroyed during
its restoration.

at Arc-et-Senans had given him the sense of a kind of "regional" or local antiquity, one that invested a place with all the authority of its own history. In Franche-Comté, introductions to local nobility and especially to the Prince de Bauffremont, "un homme de qualité" Ledoux emphasised, deepened his loyalty to a nobility with authentic titles that joined them to this antique territory. Visiting the chateau of Bauffremont at Scey-sur-Saône (Ledoux preferred the Roman appellation "Sesusone") in 1778, he was even seduced by the crenulated towers and armorial bearings of the medieval structure, the chivalric nostalgia of a fête prepared with all the mock historical accuracy of the studies of La Curne de Sainte-Palaye.[2] His project for the transformation of Bauffremont's Hunting Lodge was in severe antique style, but with its surfaces literally covered, as if painted on temporary boards or hung with tapestries deploying the armorial bearings of the prince and his hunting partners. In this architecture of illusion that merged permanent monument and temporary scene, Ledoux was to find a solution to his aesthetics of display and representation, theatrically conceived and dedicated to, in his words, a rhetoric of "persuasion."

In the invention of his modern heraldry, Ledoux not only drew liberally from his contemporaries – the iconographies of Fischer von Erlach, Piranesi and Delafosse were all absorbed – but also from Gallo-Roman precedent. Thus, the project for a triumphal arch for Cassel, far from being as the landgrave's architect reported, "in the taste of the Porte Saint-Denis," seemed to echo the Porte Noire of Besançon with its geometrically defined panels framing a rich series of allegorical bas-reliefs. Writing to Frederick II, Ledoux explained the aesthetic programme of his emblematic rhetoric: "it would be better to place bas-reliefs on the columns either in a spiral as in the Trajan column, or in rustication … by this means one can display the different traits of the life of the prince that one wishes to celebrate. One retraces his civil or heroic virtues, his alliances, his taste for the fine arts and sciences, etc." [65] Ledoux's design, which combined two monumental columns, freely adapted from Fischer's Karlskirche in Vienna, with a strictly controlled arch behind, was decorated according to Ledoux's maxim, already followed in the Saline, that "well conceived decorations should be isolated, and cannot be dominated by any part that destroys or confines them." [12] This emblem-

atic style, later developed by Ledoux into a kind of hieroglyphic code, was joined, in his urban monuments of the 1780s, to an idea of type, also influenced by his experience of Gallo-Roman antiquity, that controlled his historical allusions within a simple, easily identified model. The theatres of Besançon and Marseille, the Palace of Justice and Prisons, the governor's residence, and archbishop's palace at Aix and Sisteron, all partake of this regional typology, constructed with a mingling of respect for the traces of heroic civilisation selected for their allusive power, and a fine disregard for historical accuracy that might interfere with their adaptation to modern programmes. "The monuments of antiquity, their fragments such as they are, bear a character that commands our respect. Those of modern architects could contribute to establish the bases of instruction if they adopt whatever is good among our customs." [109]

Arc de Besançon en 1825 (d'après Clerc).

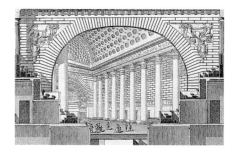

7. THEATRICAL VISION

"Our theatres are still in the infancy of art and leave much to be desired with respect to the purity of mores, solidity, health, commodity and the general effect. This last is much neglected, even though everyone knows that one of the greatest advantages of the performance is to see everything and be, in turn, well seen." [222]

The new Theatre of Besançon, while not opened to the public until 1784, and then with its decorations still incomplete, was in fact designed in tandem with the Saline de Chaux. Commissioned sometime before August 1775, the preliminary drawings were finished by the end of that year and a final model prepared by December 1776.[1] The conjunction of the two projects, the one for a theatre and the other for a manufacturing community, was of great thematic and formal importance for both; indeed Ledoux made it clear that he regarded the one as the microcosm of the other, and inserted the plans for the Besançon theatre in the first volume of *L'Architecture*, thereby emphasising the intimate link, both regional and architectural, between Saline and Theatre, theatre and utopia. The relationship was, on the most immediate level, established by the similar geometries employed: the semi-circles of *saline* and auditorium derived from those of antique theatres. But the parallel was also intended on a social level, as an analogy between the-

Left page:
Theatre of Besançon, ceiling.
From: *L'Architecture*...,
Plate 122.

Above:
Theatre of Besançon, detail of cross section.
From: *L'Architecture*...,
Plate 119.

Theatre of Besançon,
cross-sectioned
model of the interior.
Arc-et-Senans,
Musée Ledoux.

atre and society on the one hand, and as a more complex allegory of Ledoux's ideas of social and political reform and their representation, on the other. Writing to Charles-André de Lacoré, the Intendant of Franche-Comté, in August 1775, (sometime after a visit to Besançon, perhaps in conjunction with the laying of the foundation stone of the Saline), Ledoux outlined his first project for the theatre, drawings of which he enclosed. The letter, excerpts from which he inserted almost unchanged in *L'Architecture* some twenty-five years later, indicated the extent to which Ledoux was already deeply committed to the social and architectural reform of the theatre. He spoke quite seriously of his project in terms of "establishing a new religion"; "Let us return to principle," he wrote, "trampling underfoot the centuries of ignorance." More realistically, he spoke cautiously of the difficulties to overcome in a small provincial town that modelled itself on the capital; he anticipated that "at first sight, I will look like a fool, but if they want to hear me out to the end, I hope to win over the votes."[2] In fact however, while Ledoux's anticipation of opposition seemed justified in the light of the difficulties experienced by Charles de Wailly and Peyre with their similarly radical design for the Théâtre-Français (now the Odéon), the ten-year delay at Besançon was less the result of Ledoux's innovations than the product of a long-drawn out dispute between de Lacoré and

the Magistracy of the town over the proper site for the new theatre. Both Intendant and Magistracy were agreed as to the final aim: in the words of the Magistracy, to provide a building with "all the advantages that even Paris could envy, and the proportions of which should be able to fire the genius of the most talented artists of France, and, if possible, to call up antiquity before our eyes." But both parties, the independent and proud municipal government, and the representative of the French monarchy in Franche-Comté, differed profoundly on their respective definitions of the central position to be occupied by the theatre. De Lacoré, in the process of completing the new Intendancy, preferred a site close by, at the geometrical centre of that portion of Besançon enclosed by the River Doubs; he suggested a piece of land then occupied by a group of houses and shops known locally as Le Transmarchement. The Magistracy, representing the town as a whole, including the garrison and the more popular quarters on the right bank of the river, argued for a site at the centre of the town's commercial life, on the Place Neuve, next to the bridge that joined the two sides of Besançon. The subtext of this apparently aimless dispute, where the superficially subtle politics of the Intendant finally succeeded in wearing down the obstinacy of the city, was not simply one that pitted royal against local power. It concerned a fundamental division between an economic, popular view of

Théâtre de l'Odéon
by Charles de Wailly.

urban development, and an aristocratic vision of urban embellishment. The two "centres" of Besançon exactly symbolised these oppositions. The Place Neuve, an architecturally formless but socially vital commercial centre was posed against a new square that would provide a suitable back-drop for a theatre representing the civilising administration of an enlightened Intendant. But the debate also marked a decisive shift in the nature of theatricality itself. No longer was the theatre to be divided between the private quarters of an aristocratic hotel and the popular spectacle of market place, fair or tennis court; it was now to be formalised in the guise of a public monument that would confirm the place of performance in the pattern of provincial middle-class entertainment. Patronised by the royal administration and open to a hopefully well-behaved working population, the theatre was to become a specialised and professionalised realm where an "audience" in the modern sense of the term would learn to appreciate the aesthetic values of acting and the play. The crystallisation of this relatively new understanding of theatri-

cality into the building-type "theatre" was, as Ledoux recognised, to be accomplished at the expense of both popular and aristocratic traditions. For Ledoux's designs were drawn up in the context of the lively debate over the reform of the public theatre that had engaged *philosophes*, critics and architects since the late 1740s.[3] This discussion focussed not only on the proper nature of the genres – as in Voltaire's appeal to antiquity on behalf of a purified tragedy or in Diderot's definition of a bourgeois tragedy – but also on the aesthetics of the mise-en-scène and performance in the light of their social and moral effects on the audience. Diderot's concerns as to the verisimilitude of the actor, the language of gesture and the morality of the play, Rousseau's arguments against the theatre itself as a breeding place of immorality, Rétif de la Bretonne's and Sébastien Mercier's projects for reform all envisaged a new drama, a newly attentive audience and a newly formed space of theatricality; all similarly "returned" to antiquity for their models.[4] As Jean-Claude Bonnet has remarked in relation to Diderot's essays, "The concern was to renew con-

tact with antiquity by re-establishing the theatre in its pedagogic and social function. This implied a national cultural politics with acting schools and a new architecture of auditoria."[5] Such a return to antique prototypes had been envisaged by a number of architects, at least in principle, following Soufflot's decisive trip to Italy in the company of Cochin and Dumont between 1749 and 1751.[6] Soufflot, who adopted a severely modified version of the Roman amphitheatre at Lyons, Cochin, in his *Projet d'une salle de spectacle* of 1765, and Charles de Wailly in the first proposal for the Théâtre-Français of 1769 all noted the "natural" character of the antique plan, which seemed to mimic the spontaneous grouping of an audience around an entertainer on a hillside. The Roman type, excavated at Herculaneum and reported by Cochin and Bellicard as early as 1754, seemed also to avoid the principal criticism levelled against the traditional *salle*, that its rectangular form and vertical rows of *loges* prevented a proper visual relationship between audience and performance.[7] But any re-distribution of the audience inevitably had to confront the

Perspective view
of the theatre
of Besançon. From:
L'Architecture…,
Plate 115.

Below:
Theatre of Besançon,
section of the hall.
From: *L'Architecture*…,
Plate 120.

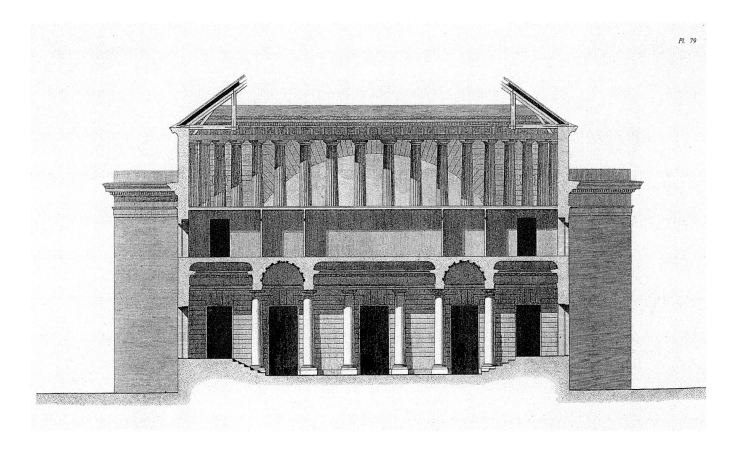

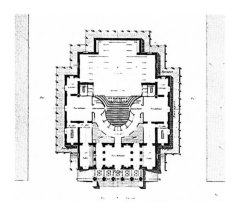 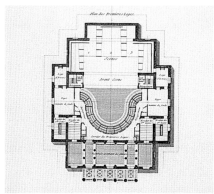 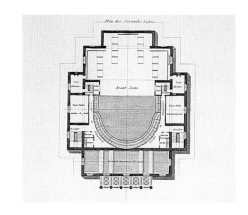

social demand for private boxes, hierarchically arranged according to criteria of fashionable display and rank, for an audience more interested in being seen than seeing, and that treated its *loges* as extensions of its salons. Ledoux was scornful of those "wooden cages," "like huge aviaries where the powers of the earth perch on their high and luxurious poles coloured like the inhabitants of the air."[220] He was equally critical of the traditional parterre or pit, the flat standing area between the first tier of boxes and the stage: it was "a sheep pen," "a deep hole where passions of every kind stir up in their slime, where the spectator's breath exhales corruption, and ceaselessly disgorges the poisons it swallows." [219] Adding to the confusion in the eyes of those who would privilege the play over the audience was the custom, still honoured in the provinces, of patronage seats on the stage itself, and an orchestra more often than not in the auditorium. Various geometrical "solutions" were advanced, ranging from the pure semi-circle, the oval, the horseshoe, the bell, to the rectilinear; arguments over acoustics, ventilation and

fire prevention complicated those over theatrical aesthetics. As Pierre Patte, sponsor of elliptical auditoria, pointed out with elaborate calculations, the assumed correspondence of the antique semi-circle to the different reforms envisaged by playwrights and moralists was difficult to prove; certainly the offence to representation posed by the quasi-egalitarian distribution of seating in the open levels of the amphitheatre was strongly resisted by the court and the aristocracy.[8] Ledoux recounted the refusal of the Abbé Terray's mistress to countenance the plans of de Wailly for this reason.

Nevertheless, Ledoux himself, supported by Trudaine, friend of Diderot and translator of Lessing, and by the passionate amateur of the theatre, the Maréchal de Duras, Governor of Franche-Comté, as well as by the enlightened de Lacoré, found little resistance to his plans, envisaged according to what he called "the progressive system." His initial arguments echoed those of Soufflot and Damun, joining natural principles to Roman precedent: "let us take for our model the simplest actions of humanity ... how, for example does one

gather in a public square around a charlatan when one wants to hear him? Everyone crowds round and surrounds him in a circle, the strongest close by and the weakest further away; but as the circle is compressed, the barker is equally well heard by all." Ledoux, taking this metaphor literally, in effect reversed the traditional order of seating: "the strongest, that is to say, he who pays the most, should be closest; ... he who pays the least should be furthest away."[9]

For his first project, only the section and a partial sketch plan of which survive, Ledoux planned an auditorium ramped in stages from an amphitheatre that took the place of the old "parterre", with seating for paying spectators, to a series of stepped-back open loges, to be occupied by the staff-officers of the garrison, rich women, and the second estate respectively, ending finally in the re-situated "parterre" in the "gods" for the poorer citizens of the town. Despite Ledoux's claims for the pure semi-circle and the authority of ancient Rome, he had thereby distorted the equally graded steps of the original model to conform, in sections and plan, at least

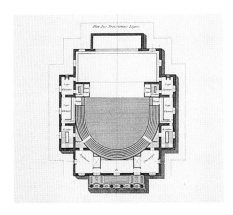
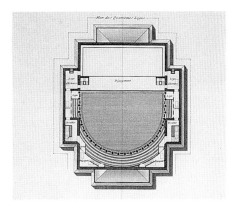

minimally, to social status. In plan, the auditorium described an open bell shape, similar to that of Charles de Wailly; above, the six rows of the new parterre achieved the pure semi-circle.

The second and final projects refined the plan and section to conform more closely to the social make-up of Besançon: the amphitheatre was renamed *le parquet*, a memory of the once privileged stage seating; the new *parterre* was divided in two by a row of Doric columns, recalling those of Palladio at Vicenza, in order to separate the soldiers of the garrison from the civil audience. As built, the theatre reified every distinction of social status and economic power: closed boxes in the proscenium for royalty and the Intendant's retinue; barred boxes beneath the gallery for rental by the year; the parquet for the rich bourgeoisie; the gallery on the same level as the royal boxes for the commanders of the garrison, officers of the police; the first row of boxes for nobles (proscribed for the bourgeoisie by order of de Lacoré); a second row of boxes for the "honest" bourgeoisie on either side, with workers and shop-girls toward the centre; a third row of

loges divided up between men and women (the parterre of the earlier projects), and, finally, rows for servants and soldiers behind the columns. These dispositions, enforced by law and marked by architectural form, served the social order of the theatre in a number of ways. First they no doubt went a long way towards filling Ledoux's initial aim "to content all the estates;" secondly, the real threat of disorderly conduct posed by the parterre had been neutralised – "the cabal will cease," stated Ledoux; thirdly, with all the audience seated, "one will be able to judge the playwrights more reasonably."[10] Ledoux was also concerned to remove what the reformers considered an inducement to immorality provided by the traditional closed boxes. Rousseau's strictures against the licentiousness of Parisian theatres, in his *Lettre à d'Alembert* (1758) and *La Nouvelle Héloïse* (1761) were echoed by the architect: "they made it a crime in Greece to build monuments to lewdness." [220] Now, displayed before the entire auditorium, the audience could not only see but be seen: transparency would, again as in Rousseau, enforce morality.[11]

From left to right:
Theatre of Besançon,
plan of the auditorium
ground floor.
From: *L'Architecture*...,
Plate 114.

Plan of the first
and second loges.
From: *L'Architecture*...,
Plate 115.

Plan of the third
and fourth loges.
From: *L'Architecture*...,
Plate 116.

THEATRICAL VISION

Theatre of Besançon,
longitudinal section.
From: *L'Architecture*...,
Plate 121.

Right page:
Theatre of Besançon,
cross section.
From: *L'Architecture*...,
Plate 119.

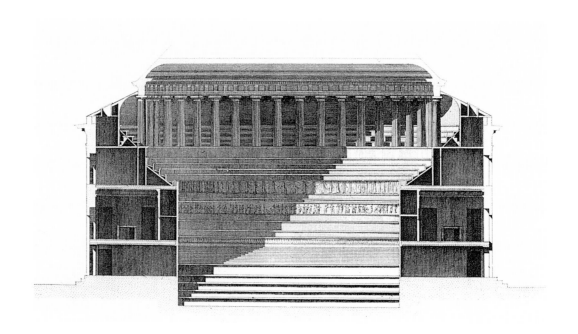

The visual advantages of the amphitheatrical plan were reinforced, in Ledoux's arguments, by its acoustical properties. Emulating the form of "the universal harmony of the world" [229], the half-spherical geometry would reflect sound proportionally through the auditorium. This revival of Renaissance harmonics, supplemented in Ledoux's project by the reverberating vases suggested by Vitruvius, was augmented by the placement of the orchestra in its own specialised realm. Ledoux designed a sunken pit between the parquet and the stage, from which the sound would be reflected by a curved wooden baffle, and which would both deepen and make more sonorous the sound, and remove any visual impediment between audience and scene – one of the earliest projects for a hidden orchestra in the modern period. With the orchestra buried, as if in anticipation of Richard Wagner's "magic gap", the audience was presented with the proscenium arch, in Ledoux's terms, the frame or window to the scene.[12] In Ledoux's imagination, the proscenium was a point of transition between the real and the fictive, society and its illusions,

and thus should, Ledoux argued, be both invisible – "a smooth element" – and a space in its own right: "the intermediary inhabited thickness that separates the action from the exterior." [221] Virtually undecorated save for bas-reliefs painted in the spandrels in imitation of the Porte Noire, its contour was conceived to emulate the curve of the eye-lid itself, while recalling the arch of one of Ledoux's bridges as it, following the Piranesian theme, framed the views beneath.

The reference to the eye is immediate and unambiguous: in the engraving of the "Coup d'oeil du Theatre de Besançon" the frame of vision is described in similar geometries, formed by the eye-lid as it cuts across the pupil and the rounded sides of the pupil itself. The engraving suggests that we are at once looking through a transparent pupil toward the empty auditorium and at the same time at a representation of its reflection. The proscenium thus focuses the gaze of actor and audience, reciprocally reflected at their point of junction. Seen through this natural frame, the stage, "the true site of magical illusions," (231) accommodated a triple scene; here Ledoux,

undoubtedly referring like Cochin in 1765, to Palladian precedent, followed de Wailly's first project which, taking its cue from the preface to Voltaire's *Sémiramis* (1748), had provided separate divisions for the presentation of three scenes simultaneously.[13] Ledoux, however, removed the separating columns in the Théâtre-Français project, and unified his three scenes beneath a single arch, implying the inter-relations of each part of the tableau to the whole. Dard de Bosco, the stage engineer, confessed his frustration at this "mad idea" of the architect, but admitted its novelty.[14] Ledoux himself contributed designs for some of the sets, notably those for a salon and gallery, a public square, and, most striking of all, the one depicted in the engraved cross-section. Here, framed by the rusticated proscenium, a stage-set representing a huge basilican hall, with a colonnade of giant Corinthian pillars and a coffered barrel-vault, is deployed in diagonal perspective. But, to the rear, replacing the expected apsidal ending to the basilica, Ledoux has substituted a depiction of the amphitheatrical auditorium itself seen through

a reflected image of the proscenium. The audience is thus presented, so to speak, with a redoubled image of itself, a mirror image of the auditorium on the stage.

The explanation of this ingenious illusion is provided by Ledoux's adherence to a tradition of representation whereby the published engraving of a theatrical project showed the stage as set for the formal opening of the theatre. In the case of Besançon, this took place in August 1784, in the presence of the Prince de Condé, Governor of Burgundy, and his son, the Duc de Bourbon. In the words of the Hôtel de Ville register, the opening performance presented "a production analogous to the presence of their majesties themselves," that is, a dramatic performance mimicking the opening ceremony.[15] Thence the reflected auditorium in Ledoux's back-drop, and thence also the steep diagonal perspective that allowed those seated in the royal box, the prince and the duke, to be placed on axis with the fictive auditorium. In the event, Ledoux's semi-circular geometry proved too strong, even for the distinguished visitors who, "after having seen and

examined their boxes, preferred to seat themselves in the middle of the gallery in front of the stage."[16] Ledoux's theatrical analogy did not simply, as Daniel Rabreau has pointed out, refer to the conditions of Besançon, however.[17] His understanding of the theatre as a microcosm of the city was perfectly expressed in this image of an audience extended, so to speak, into the city by way of the scenery, only to be re-doubled and closed on itself by its own image as audience, in a theatre that represented a city in microcosm. Over thirty years after the completion of the Besançon theatre, Karl Friedrich Schinkel adopted the same device in his own painted back-drop for the inauguration of the Schauspielhaus in Berlin.[18] The perspective was there calculated from the central position of the King in the auditorium, and showed the opera house itself exactly as it would have appeared from the King's private apartments in his palace, provided, of course, that all the intervening buildings had been cleared away. Like Ledoux, and in an equally complex manner, Schinkel thus integrated his perspectival vision of the urban landscape into this privileged "royal"

vision. Ledoux's vision, as the *coup d'oeil* showed, was less picturesque than it was social: for Ledoux the theatre, in order to escape the total prohibition of Rousseau and to take its place in a world of moralising institutions, was primarily to be a place of "public instruction." Assembled in tiers around the hemi-cycle, the public would at once learn from the moral tableaux on the scene, and from their own spectacle, each estate dressed according to its means, each placed according to its powers. Ledoux, like Rousseau, but with opposite intent, took his cue from the image of popular spectacles, where on the steps of a temporary wooden stadium a vast crowd would gather naturally in the open air, the people as their own theatre: "It is there … where man, returned to his primitive state, will find again the equality he should never have lost. It is in this vast theatre, balanced in the clouds, circles above circles, that he partakes of the secrets of the Gods." [223] Obeying the circular laws of nature, literally seated "in the gods", the audience would, through mimesis, retrieve its lost natural state: this is the central motif that joins the series

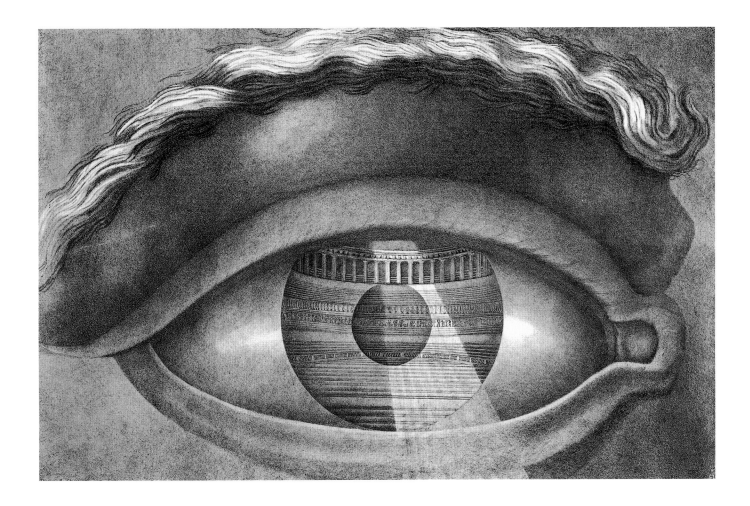

Left page:
Theatre
of Besançon.

Above:
"Coup d'œil"
of the theatre
of Besançon.
From: *L'Architecture…*,
Plate 113.

of allegorical engravings of *L'Architecture* – the "Coup d'oeil of the theatre" [Pl. 113] as the culmination of, on the one hand, the engraving of "L'abri du pauvre" [Pl. 33], where "savage man," naked and alone, shivering beneath a tree, implores the gods assembled in the clouds above for aid, and the "Élévation du cimétière" [Pl. 100], on the other hand, depicting the universe in astronomical and zodiacal orbits, the earth half submerged in clouds. As if to reinforce this microcosmic place of the theatre, the ceiling of the auditorium of Besançon, designed by Ledoux, depicted, as if painted on an awning drawn over an open-air theatre, Apollo and his attendants rising with a gilded sun at the centre of a circle that completed that of the theatre. No doubt

Ledoux, imagining his role as architect, providing for the poor and sheltering the dead while instructing the living, found pleasure in this emblem of the artist as sun god, coupled with the symbol of the Roi-Soleil whose classical monuments Ledoux had evoked with nostalgia. In the unbuilt project for the theatre of Marseille, Ledoux again placed Apollo and his chariot, drawn by a quadriga, above the pedimented entrance.[19]

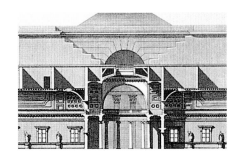

8. PHYSIOGNOMIES OF JUSTICE

"Laws come to the aid of mores. The enlightened temple of justice forms a salutary opposition to the sombre lairs of crime that should never harbour innocence." [3]

If, in the theatre of Besançon, Ledoux had been able to frame a return to antiquity within a suitable contemporary guise, in the projects for the new Palais de Justice of Aix-en-Provence, he was confronted with a difficult and unavoidable choice between antiquity and modernism: between the protection of an historical structure that incorporated significant Roman remains in its fabric, and its destruction in favour of a new building.[1] The old Palais de Justice that had housed the Parlement of Provence from 1501, and before then had served as the fortified palace of the Comtes de Provence, was marked by the presence of three Roman towers, the traces of the foundation of Aquae Sextiae. One was square, and thought to be a mausoleum, the other two were round, and flanked the old gate through the ramparts; all were well-recognised symbols of the authority of the city's Gallo-Roman foundation. The palace itself, seat of the three chambers of parliament – the Grand'Chambre, the Chambre de La Tournelle and the Chambre des Enquêtes – also housed the private apartments of the Governor of Provence, the offices of the Cour des Comptes, the Bureau des Finances, the Sénéchaussée, and the prisons, together with

Left page:
Palais de Justice,
Aix-en-Provence,
roof plan.
From: *L'Architecture*…,
Ramée edition,
Plate 52.

Above:
Palais de Justice,
Aix-en-Provence,
section detail.
From: *L'Architecture*…,
Ramée edition,
Plate 57.

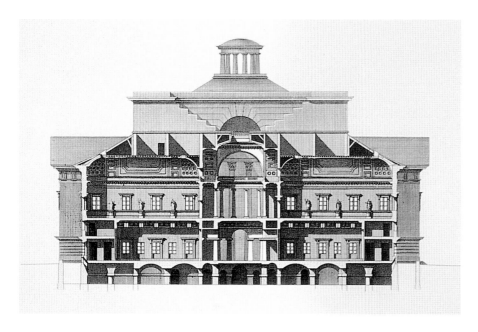

Palais de Justice,
Aix-en-Provence,
section.
From: *L'Architecture*...,
Ramée edition,
Plate 57.

Right page:
Palais de Justice,
Aix-en-Provence,
ground floor plan.
From: *L'Architecture*...,
Ramée edition, Plate 46.

their respective audience chambers and chapels. Standing at the centre of a group of public institutions in the old Bourg and Ville Comtale, – the Hôtel de Ville, the cathedral of Saint-Sauveur, the archbishop's palace, and the university – the Palais de Justice stood as the emblem of Aix's position as site of the provincial government and first town of Provence.[2] But the building was, as the parliamentarians realised on their return from Maupeou's three years of enforced exile in 1775, in a dangerous state of disrepair; survey's were conducted by a local architect, and in 1776 Ledoux himself was called to Aix at the invitation of the Intendant and the recommendation of Turgot and Trudaine de Montigny.[3] His report cited water damage and unstable foundations, and, by 1778, he had drawn up a project for a new parliament building, re-sited on open land outside the old walls, to the south-west of the Bourg and at the end of the promenade known as the Cours. To connect the palace to the centre he envisaged the extension of the Cours at the east end, forming a wide avenue across the town, framed at one end by the parliament and at the other

by a triumphal arch.[4] This dramatic attempt to apply the precepts of Enlightenment embellishment to Aix was, together with Ledoux's two other projects of 1779 and 1783 which equally avoided the site of the old palace in favour of less restricted plots outside the walls, rejected out of hand by the Assemblée des Communautés de Provence as the intrusion of a "foreigner" and too costly.

Behind this refusal of Ledoux's projects, however, as he was later to realise, was more than a simple assertion of local pride, or even of economic necessity; rather it asserted the allegiance of the parliament to the old building, or at least to its position in the city. A move to the periphery would relinquish this privileged site, the focus of festivals and ceremonies, the back-drop for carnival and ritual. The traditional fêtes described by Achard in his *Description historique de Provence* (1787), or the ceremonials of Corpus Christi analysed historically by Grégoire in 1777, established the palace at the centre of a closed network of streets and monuments that served as the frame for public processionals and

bazoches, or local carnivals, alike.[5] Nevertheless, against this traditional affection, the rumours had it, there emerged a certain pleasure in the demolition of a building that had housed a rival parliament, even if only for four years; certainly, many parliamentarians and their friends stood to gain financially from the redevelopment of an area in which they owned property.[6] Indeed, by 1784, a majority was evidently in favour of the complete reconstruction of the palace, supported by Calonne's decision, as minister of Finances, to contribute two thirds of the cost from the royal treasury. Demolition, tentatively started in 1776, was hastened, and the foundations of Ledoux's new palace begun in 1787.

Faced with the imminent disappearance of the old Palais Comtale, as the research of Serge Conard has demonstrated, there emerged a current of conservationist opposition led by local antiquarians and historians, a number of whom were themselves distinguished members of parliament: the President, Fauris de Saint-Vincens, the lawyer Charles-François Bouche and the painter Esprit Gibelin were among those who

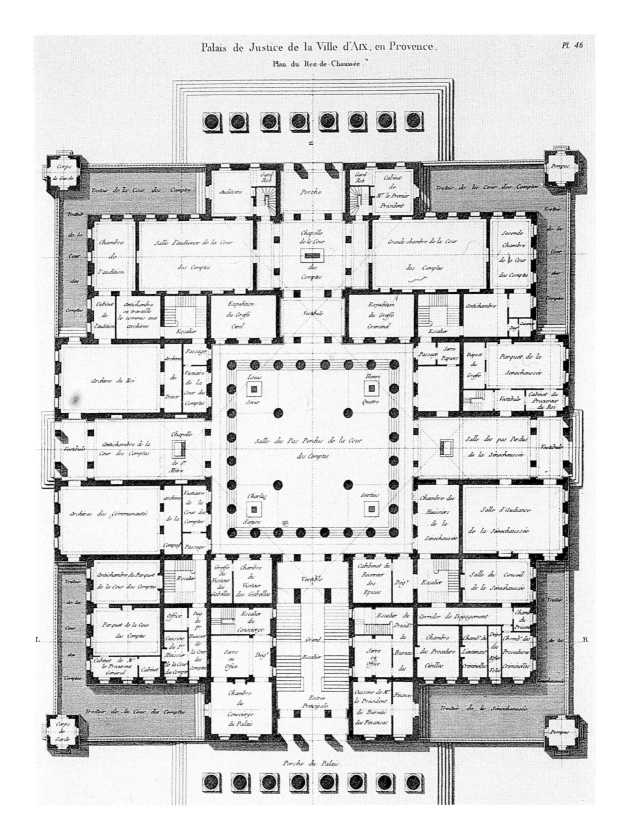

Palais de Justice de la Ville d'Aix, en Provence.

Plan du Rez-de-Chaussée.

Pl. 46

Left page:
Palais de Justice
and prison,
Aix-en-Provence,
general plan.
From: *L'Architecture*…,
Ramée edition,
Plate 44.

voiced their anger at the destruction of the palace, and especially of the Roman towers.[7] Saint-Vincens and Gibelin followed the course of the demolition with archaeological interest, while Bouche, in a series of reports in 1785 and 1787, castigated the decision to replace the ancient monuments with the ephemeral and "light" products of what he called "modern architecture." If it were not possible to save the towers in the manner used by the Greeks – re-locating them by transporting their stones – he proposed a memorial to their former existence composed of bronze columns mounted on blocks of marble: a fitting recognition of the first masons of Aix by this eighteenth-century freemason, and a first stage in the long campaign for the preservation of a French patrimony.[8]

Ledoux, aware of the belated movement for preservation, was unconcerned. Writing to his friend and contractor Mignard in 1786 on the subject of the remains discovered in the base of the mausoleum, he observed dryly, "with respect to the urn … I think that it is good to look at, but its uninteresting form can only please those who collect in their *cabinets des antiquités*."[9] Certainly, while he had avoided building over the old palace for as long as possible, he had no feeling for the towers as works of architecture: their interest was solely archaeological. Like d'Alembert and the *philosophes* in their scorn of antiquarians, Ledoux was entirely confident

in the ability of his own "philosophical" architecture to compete with that of Rome.

Ledoux's design for the Palais de Justice nevertheless attempted to address the "historical" nature of its context and predecessor on two levels: that of the spatial organisation of the complex programme and of the symbolic representation in architecture of the monumental history of Aix. In the first place, Ledoux was careful to preserve the traditional relationships between the different courts; arrangements that while originally the result of haphazard growth had necessarily become embodied in the rituals and forms of parliament. Thus, the hierarchy of the courts had placed the Cour des Comptes with its chapel and Salle des Pas-Perdus on the ground floor and the parliament with its three courts, Salles des Pas-Perdus and Salles d'Audience on the first floor, reached by a grand stair from the east entrance.[10] Ledoux adopted this vertical division, articulating it in plan and section so as to heighten the sense of spatial ceremony; a comparison of Ledoux's design with the detailed account by Grégoire of the week-long Fête-Dieu would even suggest that the architect was well aware of the needs of the traditional *bazoche*. Similarly, the lower offices of the Senéchaussée and the Bureau des finances, squeezed between prison and parliament in the old palace, were accommodated by Ledoux in the mezzanine. Finally, the prisons themselves, originally built

behind the Roman wall connecting the two round towers, seem, in Ledoux's treatment, to have been literally "detached" from their former position and reinstalled in the form of four corner towers in an isolated building to the rear of the palace.

On the level of architectural expression as well, Ledoux made overt reference to the demolished palace and, more generally, to the historical monuments of Aix. While the efforts of Serge Conard to demonstrate Ledoux's "assimilation" of the traces of the old towers in the geometries of his plan seem unconvincing, given the complete lack of two or three-dimensional correspondences, symbolic references are more evident. Conard points out the similarity between the fifteenth-century drawing of the palace by Giuliano da Sangallo and Ledoux's layout of palace and prisons, but the resemblance of the upper rotunda of the mausoleum, as depicted by Gibelin, to Ledoux's temple-like lantern of the Palais de Justice is also striking.[11] This latter motif might equally recall another mythical monument of Aix, the Temple du Soleil, supposedly surviving in the semi-circle of antique Corinthian columns in the baptistery of the cathedral of Saint-Sauveur. This said, however, Ledoux's designs were hardly historicist. Rather, they were more concerned with the representation of their late eighteenth-century roles, self-contained exemplars of a new type than with any eclectic citations. The play of the square and Greek cross in the Palais de Justice re-stated a monumental theme taken up in the same period in the public baths and church of Chaux, while the great central stair, divided at ground level to provide access to the Comptes and joined at the mezzanine to prepare for the Grande Salle, mounted diagonally towards the chapel, much in the same way as that of the Maison du Directeur of the Saline. Ledoux thus deployed his spatial vocabulary of public types so as at once to provide a "family resemblance" among all his projects for institutions, while responding to the different hierarchical needs of the judiciary. What Ledoux was later to call "le temple éclairé de la justice" or "le prétoire" in memory of its Roman origins, emerged as a complex synthesis of antique types and motifs, Palladian compositional geometries and his own, ready-formed, institutional language. Juridical tradition was installed in a combination "basilica," ancient seat of the law, and "temple", that recalled the "Druidical" temple installed by legend in Aix.

The same was not true for the project for the prisons, where, in 1784, Ledoux could draw on few typological precedents save for the host of iconographical experiments following the Carceri of Piranesi that had extended the spatial language of imprisonment to new pictorial levels. Apart from these explorations of the "terrible sublime," the appropriate genre identified by Blondel for prisons, there had been little attention to the programmatic needs of a prison equal to that, say, for the hospital in the same period.[12] A commission of enquiry into the Parisian prisons, appointed by Necker and led by Tenon, had opened a minor debate; Moreau, then Boullée, had proposed alterations to the Hôtel de la Force; the Académie had included the subject in its programme for 1778. But the influential catalogue assembled by John Howard in the same year had not yet received distribution in France, and no proposals like those of Antoine Petit, Bernard Poyet or Le Roy for the Hôtel-Dieu had caught the public imagination. Ledoux's prison, indeed, seems to stand apart in the 1780s as a self-conscious attempt to address programmatic and expressive problems for a reformed incarceration. Here Ledoux seems to have been guided by the criteria of Brissot de Warville, whose *Théorie des lois criminelles*, published in 1781, described a model prison that corresponds exactly to that of Ledoux's.[13] Like Ledoux's, Brissot's "maison de correction" was four stories high and conceived a perfect square divided into four parts, each specified for a kind of inmate – women and children, debtors, libertines, and murderers or convicted criminals awaiting death or deportation. Each had its own workshops, infirmaries and exercise courtyards. The chapel was in the middle. On the expressive level, however, Ledoux went further than Brissot who simply pre-

scribed "une épigraphe terrible" over the main door. Ledoux provided this with the inscription "Securitas publica," but he also attempted to invent a rhetoric that would, without falling into the excesses of the Piranesians, unambiguously denote the building's function. Profiting from a visit to the private museum of the anatomist Jean Tournatory, whose lugubrious collection of pathology, osteology and criminology had

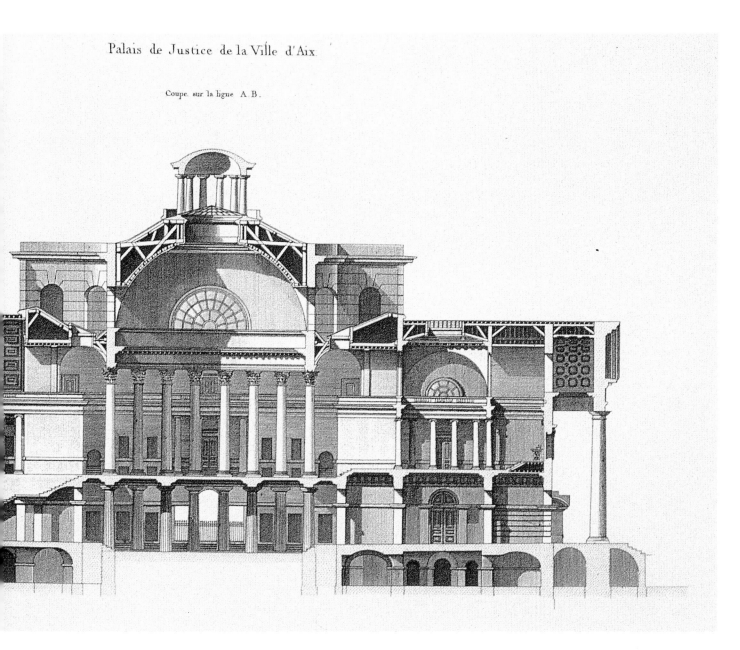

Palais de Justice de la Ville d'Aix

Coupe sur la ligne A.B.

become celebrated in Aix long before the doctor had been appointed Professor of Anatomy
in the Faculty of Medicine, Ledoux applied the
notion of physiognomy to the facades of his prisons.[14] Alluding to the revival of this art of reading character from faces, popularised in the
1780s by the writings of Lavater and re-incor-
porated into architectural theory, first by Blondel
and then, more directly, by Le Camus de Méz-

ières, Ledoux drew the analogy between the
expressive nature of Tournatoris's collection of
heads, each signalling the criminal mentality of
their former owners, and the design of the
prison.[15]
The heavy, lowering walls, slit-like "eyes" and forbidding entry clearly indicated "the dark places
intended for crime." But Ledoux avoided the more
literal transcriptions of facial character on

Palais de Justice,
Aix-en-Provence,
section.
From: *L'Architecture*…,
Ramée edition,
Plate 55.

Following double page:
Model of the Palais
de Justice and prison,
Aix-en-Provence.
Arc-et-Senans,
Musée Ledoux.

PHYSIOGNOMIES OF JUSTICE

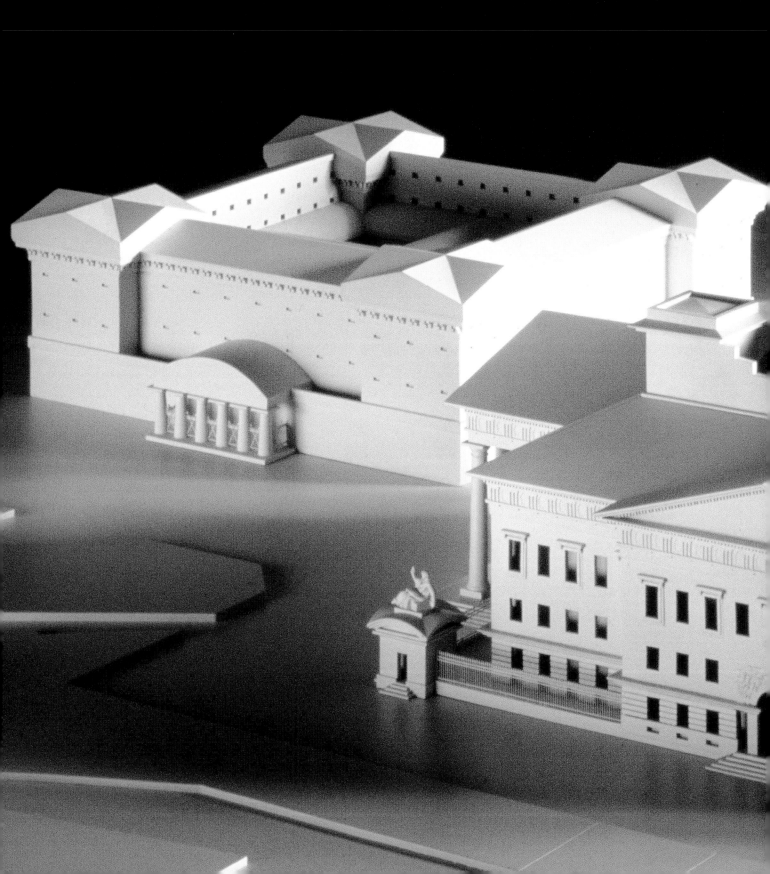

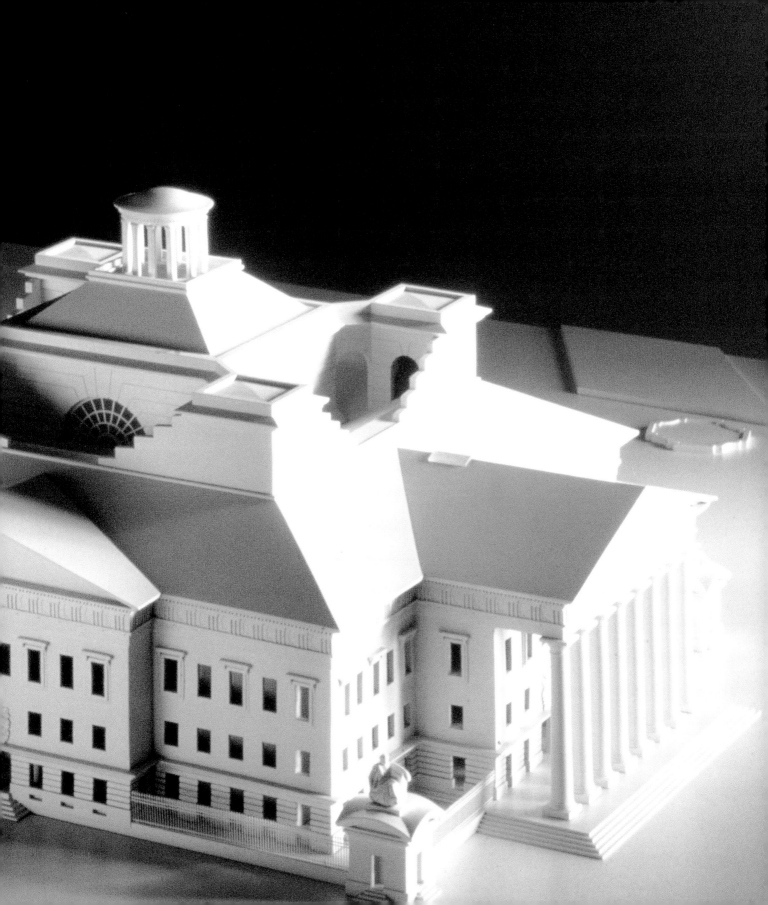

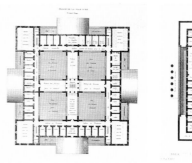
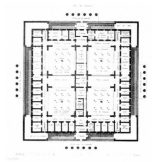

facades practiced by caricature artists, such as Jean-Jacques Lequeu early in the next century, by utilising purely architectural motifs to gain his effect. His references were to the funereal architecture of antiquity, filtered through an abstracting geometry: the cellular interior, which Conard has recognised as an image of the catacombs of Pozzuoli, the "tomb stones" of the corner towers, and the tomb-slab pediment over the entry, itself from Pozzuoli by way of the caprices of Delafosse, were all welded into a composition that seems to be carved from a single block of stone, a primitive sepulchre for the condemned.[16] When finally published by Daniel Ramée in 1846, this image became immediately a sign of physiognomic architecture, selected by Charles Blanc as an example of a monument that "through its savage beauty, its fierce appearance," and its use of dominant plane surfaces was a veritable primer of the terrible sublime.[17]

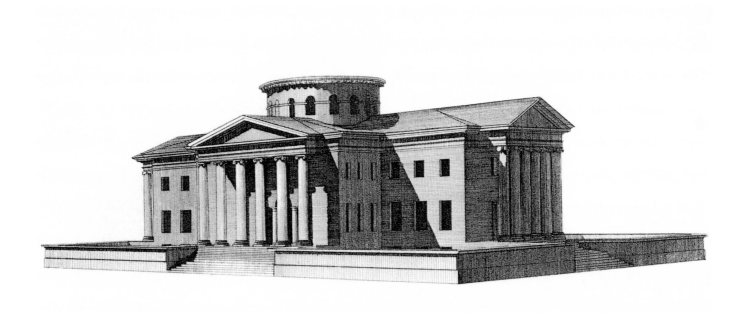

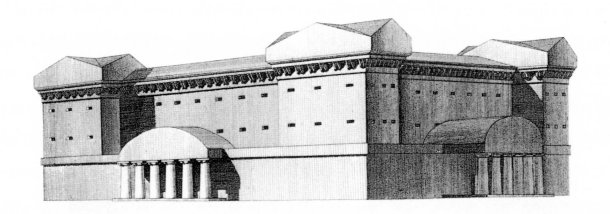

9. FROM TOLLGATES TO PROPYLAEA

"I will present the Propylaea of Paris, as they were before their mutilation, views that are joined to the liveliest sites and whose effects are close to the illusory effects of our theatres." [18]

None of Ledoux's designs, projected or built, were so immediately and consistently the objects of outrage, criticism and condemnation as were the tollgates or *barrières* of Paris.[1] Erected in the last years of the Ancien Régime in secrecy and haste, they were inevitably seen as the visible emblems of fiscal tyranny, enforced by the hated Ferme Générale. Their monumentality and strange forms, exaggerating traditional architectural motifs in scale and placement to the point of caricature, seemed to confirm the economic profligacy of the regime. They were attacked by latter-day Physiocrats as epitomising a useless investment in urban embellishment and the evils of a monopoly system of centralised taxation; by reform ministers as denying by their very cost the benefits they were built to collect; by journalists who seized on their bizarre forms as objects around which to rally criticism of the government and its agents; by a wide-ranging coalition of special interests (the tavern keepers outside the old city boundary whose profits in untaxed wine were undermined, as well as wine traders, legal and illegal); by the proprietors of expropriated lands; and, finally, by architects and

Left page:
Bureau de Pantin,
also Rotonde
de la Villette,
detail of columns.

Above:
Rotonde
de la Villette.

critics for their outrageous flouting of all classical canons.[2] What for Ledoux and a small circle of loyal friends and protectors represented the height of his aspirations as an architect, uniting the general amelioration of the outskirts, the development of new boulevards and the monumental embellishment of every quarter – a truly "Roman" project – became in a very short time the cause of his disgrace, downfall and the basis of his subsequent reputation as an "architecte maudit." The immediate source of conflict, one that haunted Ledoux throughout his life, but that was here brought into sharp aesthetical-political focus, was his self-acknowledged propensity for architectural overstatement and hyperbole, for elevating modest subjects by their architectural treatment. His principle, clearly stated in the introduction to *L'Architecture*, was to offer "for

the smallest object that which the greatest admits;" in the case of the *barrières* this led to their redefinition from small offices for the agents of the Ferme to triumphal entries for the city – "clerks' offices become … magnificent Propylaea." [16] What in Laugier's description of 1753 had been no more than "a few miserable palisades, roughly set up on wooden railings, swinging on two old hinges and flanked by two or three piles of manure," were now re-conceived according to Le Roy's images of the gate to the Acropolis.[3] Where Laugier complained that strangers entering Paris were unable to believe they were not still "in some neighbouring village," Ledoux promised: "I will "de-villagerise" a population of eight-hundred thousand in order to give it the independence that a town possesses in its isolation; I will set up trophies of victory where now

the closed exits destroy the lines of sight." [18] But Ledoux's adherence to Laugier's general programme rested there; while the *philosophe* had called for entirely traditional entries to the city – "grand triumphal arches" set in the middle of vast squares from which radiated the streets of the capital – Ledoux, rejecting the traditional type as both functionally and aesthetically inadequate, gave himself the freedom to invent a new form of entry. For Laugier, Nicolas-François Blondel's seventeenth-century Porte Saint-Denis was the model, the more so as it rejected the Roman habit of mingling columns with arcades: columns, in his view, carried with them the idea of "dwelling houses," as opposed to a triumphal arch which "can only be a place of passage."[4] But for Ledoux, presented with a programme that precisely mixed the function of dwelling with that of triumphal

passage, neither the Roman nor the seventeenth-century type was appropriate. In the event, the motif of the triumphal arch properly speaking hardly appeared at all, and, as his critics were quick to point out, Ledoux was certainly not averse to the abundant use of columns.

The need for a new fiscal *enceinte* for Paris had been estimated in 1782 by the Farmer General and scientist Lavoisier: a more permanent boundary than that erected after the demolition of the old ramparts in 1672 would, he calculated, save some six million livres in lost revenues; he proposed the building of a wall beginning with an enclosure of the south-eastern districts of the Hôpital Générale, the Salpêtrière, Vaugirard, Gros-Caillou, the École Militaire and the Invalides.[5] In this plan the tightening of fiscal control was evidently also associated with that of

social police; the quarters around the Salpêtrière were notorious centres of criminal life, and their *guinguettes*, or local inns, brought together the unemployed, the destitute and the petty criminal: the *classe laborieuse* and the *classe dangereuse*. Tabled under Necker, the scheme was revived under Calonne and developed into a grand project for the amelioration and control of the Parisian *faubourgs*. As presented to the city of Paris in early 1784, it consisted of not only the new wall and its gates, but also offices and dwellings for a staff of over eight hundred employees of the Ferme, including a guard of *chasseurs* for policing the boundary and clerks and receivers to assess and collect the dues. This force was to be distributed around the wall according to the relative importance of each entrance. A typical gate would provide living and sleeping quarters

for a brigade of seven guards, an *avant-garde* of four or five with their brigadier, rooms for a clerk and receiver, kitchens, offices, cellars for wine and wood storage. Separate sentry boxes would shelter the officers on duty to either side of the gate. Supplementing these *barrières* were warehouses for confiscated goods, customs sheds, observation posts, stables and carriage houses. These functions were divided among fifty-five points of entry, and joined by an encircling boulevard that isolated the wall outside and inside the city boundary and provided continuous circulation round the perimeter. Building started in 1785, and despite the temporary suspension of Ledoux as architect in 1787 and his permanent removal in 1789 almost all of the forty-five projected *barrières* of Ledoux were completed before his death in 1806 when he might see, not with-

Preceding
double page
Left:
Model of the Barrière
des Réservoirs.
Arc-et-Senans,
Musée Ledoux.

Right:
Model of the
Barrière de la Villette.
Arc-et-Senans,
Musée Ledoux.

out bitterness for his unpaid work, sixty-two of his designs for monumental office buildings with their accompanying sentry boxes standing in a great circle around Paris.[6]

Some of these *barrières* were modest – two rooms in a single-story pavilion – some extensive and several stories high, but all were invested with a similar architectural character, fabricated as it were out of a versatile kit of parts, abstracted by Ledoux out of Renaissance and antique prototypes, with apparently infinite properties for combination and re-combination. The plan-types selected by Ledoux were simple enough and few in number: amphiprostyle and peripteral temples; the Greek cross in a square, playing all the variations on Palladio's Villa Rotunda; cubic pavilions with pediments on two or four faces; pavilions with rusticated porticoes attached; circular rotundas, and combinations of two or more of these. The set of architectural elements was also reduced to a minimum: Venetian openings for windows and doors, sometimes linked in series with single or double columns; a primitive Doric order, generally unfluted and baseless with an exaggerated entasis taken from Paestum; rustication liberally used for podia, ground stories and bases, applied to columns as reticulation round or square; pediments, sometimes broken by Serliana, sometimes abstracted out of the form of gables, sometimes segmental, sometimes invaded by dramatically projecting keystones. These basic elements were mustered in order to generate a series of pavilions, single or paired, that responded to the different character of their sites while joined in a family resemblance as buildings of the Ferme.[7]

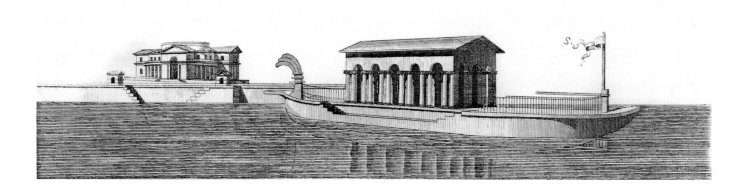

Left page:
Perspective view
of the Bureau
de la Rapée with
the patache in the
foreground. From:
L'Architecture…,
Ramée edition, Plate 14.

Below:
Patache de la Rapée,
model of a side elevation.
Arc-et-Senans,
Musée Ledoux.

The more important entries were marked by major building complexes, significant commissions in their own right. To the north, the Barrières of La Villette and Pantin were supplemented by a large customs house: the Bureau Saint-Martin, with its high central rotunda enclosing an open courtyard (on the model of Le Camus de Mézières's Halle au Blé) and surrounded by Venetian arches, set on a square base and entered through four equal porticoes with pediments and square Tuscan columns. The customs house and observation post of the Barrière d'Enfer was built in the form of a rotunda topped by a cylindrical flat-domed lantern and entered through three porches with pedimented gables and rusticated *veneziane*. To east and west, the river gates were controlled by custom's boats or *pataches* operating from the Barrière de la Cunette and the customhouse of Quai de la Rapée. At La Cunette, the gate took the form of a wide-gabled pediment over three Venetian arches on doubled rusticated columns, and was entered at river level from a basin sheltering the pataches through a heavily rusticated, grotto-like archway. The Barrière de la Rapée was a circular building with an open central courtyard and an external peristyle of baseless Doric, entered beneath four porches whose gabled pediments were decorated with projecting keystones. For this *barrière* Ledoux also prepared a design for the *patache*, in the form of a peripteral temple surrounded by linked Venetian arches built on a kind of neo-classical gondola – the Palladian temple brought back to its origins, so to speak.

These functionally important *barrières* were balanced in scale and magnificence by the symbol-

Barrière
de Monceau,
elevation.
From: *L'Architecture*…,
Ramée edition,
Plate 4.

Right page:
Barrière
de Monceau,
Monceau Park,
Paris.

ically more important "Royal" entries, the designs for which Ledoux had to submit for Louis XVI's approbation. To the west, the entry from Versailles along the Quai des Bonshommes was marked by a free-standing pavilion, with a semicircular coffered porch, like that at the Hôtel Guimard, fronted by a screen of Doric columns. Intimating the great east-west axis, yet to be realised, the double pavilions of the Barrière de l'Étoile and the Barrière de Vincennes or du Trône – the former with their facades borrowed from the Maison de Directeur of the Saline de Chaux, the latter flanking two free-standing monumental Doric columns on cruciform bases – completed Ledoux's not entirely altruistic homage to the monarchy. In his justificatory memoranda Ledoux recorded the roles of d'Angeviller, Directeur des Bâtiments Royaux, and Calonne in the design of these gates. For the Champs-Élysées (then the Avenue de Neuilly), "The King desired that the *barrières* … important for their position, should herald the Place Louis XV and the entrance to the Louvre."[8] Accordingly, d'Angeviller offered advice on character, and on the appropriate iconography for the pavilions of the Étoile. Ledoux's comments on the style of the *barrières* confirmed his general approach toward the creation of a new public genre of architecture: he was, he wrote, "content to present the needs of the Farm with a regular, masculine, and understated order." Writing three months later on the

same subject, he affirmed: "the artist is content to endow these offices with a public character and, so that the architecture not be lost to sight and diminished in these immense spaces, he has believed it best to use the most severe and unambiguous style."[9] These marks of a style specifically calculated at once to represent a public *enceinte* for the city and the attributes of a monopolistic corporation dependent on royal authority were consistently employed throughout the other *barrières*. The adoption of classical types gave the wall a Roman aspect – the via Appia seen through the eyes of Piranesi – while the re-quotation of motifs already used for the Ferme's earlier buildings at Chaux and in the Hôtel des Fermes stamped the whole with its unmistakeable ownership. But Ledoux was also exploring the limits of a new form of classicism, creating new entities out of the dismembered fragments of the old. What gave all the *barrières* their unity was Ledoux's commitment to a radical form of primitivism that, derived equally from Le Roy and Piranesi, Athens and Paestum, was joined to the idea of origins by its geometrical reductivism. In the context of the similarly primitive, Tuscan back-drops to the heroic paintings by Jacques-Louis David in the same years – perhaps themselves derived from an observation of Ledoux's mature manner – it is possible to speak of a style of the mid-1780s entirely distinct from its more elegant predecessors (theo-

rised by Laugier and practised by Soufflot and Gondouin) as well as from its more historicist successors (theorised by Quatremère de Quincy and practised by Durand). This primitivism, also espoused by Brongniart and de Wailly, and later in England by John Soane, was, as the critic Legrand realised, the personal invention of Ledoux. Thus the various temple-*barrières* were conceived as transformations of an original type at once less purist and more architectonic than that of Laugier. Best represented by Ledoux's project for the Barrière des Rats, it consisted of a peripteral temple in plan, with square "Etruscan" columns of stocky proportions, without bases and with only rudimentary capitals. These carried a gabled roof without architrave or frieze that echoed Inigo Jones's restorations of Vitruvius's Tuscan temple. A next stage of development was designed for the Barrière de Courcelles, a peripteral, hexastyle temple in a Doric order, baseless, unfluted and without frieze, an order repeated in the tetrastyle porticoes of the small amphiprostyle temple at the Barrière de l'Oursine. Other versions were built at the Barrières de Bercy, Saint-Mandé, Montreuil and Charenton. If these primitive "types" seemed offensive to critics imbued with a nascent sense of neo-classical historicism, then Ledoux's introduction of *veneziane* and other Palladian motifs into the temple model presented, as Quatremère de Quincy was to recognise, a species of "monster" to crit-

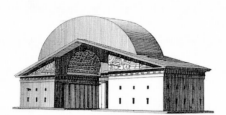

Fragments des Propylées.

Vue Perspective.

Fragments
of the Propylaea
of Paris. From:
L'Architecture…,
Ramée edition,
Plate 29.

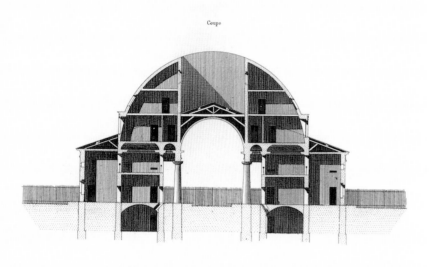

Coupe

Elevation.

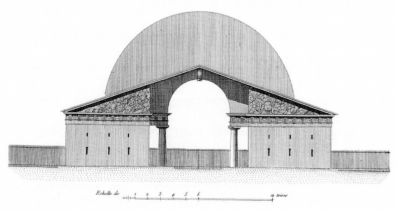

Echelle de 1 2 3 4 5 6   14 toises

Le Doux Architecte du Roi   Gravé par Van …

ical opinion. Directly opposed to Laugier's austere rejection of the combination of arch and column, Ledoux played with every variation of the linked Venetian arch, sometimes on single columns to form porticoes, as at the Barrière de Clichy, or used on double columns, as at Belleville. Here Ledoux created a type somewhere between the temple and the basilica, between the sacred and the profane. In its perfect, peripteral form, it was built at Menilmontant, with three arches on double unfluted columns to a side. Even more Palladian in inspiration, were a series of *barrières* conceived as variations on the Villa Rotunda, freely employing the Greek cross-in-square plan, sometimes with a central lantern, cylindrical, domed or square, sometimes with pedimented or vaulted porches, as in the large Barrière du Roule, the Barrières de Vaugirard, des Trois-Couronnes and de la rue Royale-Montmartre with their varieties of Venetian porches, and the Barrière de Picpus, with pedimented porches of unfluted Doric opening onto semi-circular porches. In many of the *barrières*, Ledoux's model was more simply that of the private hôtel, entered through monumental porticoes: those of the Place d'Italie with their continuous arcades to shelter the customs agents at work; the two pavilions of the Barrière d'Enfer, their triple Venetian arches on double columns heavily banded by rustication; the Barrière Saint-Denis, originally designed as a pedi-

Fragments
of the Propylaea
of Paris, Chemin
de Saint-Denis.
From: *L'Architecture...*,
Ramée edition,
Plate 5.

Fragments des Propylées de Paris, chemin de St. Denis.

Premier Projet.

Elévations Latérales.

mented peristyle joining two detached pavilions; the Barrières de Fontarabie and du Maine, in the latter of which the entrances were surmounted by stepped blocks of rustication, a motif borrowed directly from the Hôtel des Fermes itself. Other *barrières* were less directly modelled on existing types, and simply presented varieties of pedimented, cubic pavilions – the École Militaire and the Place de Vincennes. Others nested double pediments, some broken, some segmental as at the Barrières des Paillassons, des Vertus or Sainte-Marie and de Chaillot. Some, recalling garden *fabriques*, and generally used by Ledoux in open, park-like settings, took the form of pure rotundas: the observation post of d'Enfer, the Barrière des Amandiers in the quarter of market-gardens, the Barrière de Neuilly with its pure peristyle of eighteen arches on columns, and, of course, the Rotonde de Chartres, conceived expressly for the decoration of the Duc d'Orléans's garden of Monçeau and containing his private apartment on the top floor. Another, smaller group of *barrières* took their model, as Legrand remarked, from the wayside tombs and chapels of Italy – a nostalgia that Ledoux could only have shared with his contemporaries by way of Piranesi – those of Saint-Jacques, Montparnasse, des Ministres and des Martyrs. Finally, Ledoux projected, but did not build, three gates in the form of triumphal arches, albeit of a kind unknown in Italy: the Bar-

rière Poissonnière and two others published by Ramée show gabled buildings cut by wide arches through their short axis forming arcaded galleries lit from above by circular lanterns. In these last projects, no doubt engraved after the Revo-

lution, Ledoux's style approached that of the ideal designs for Chaux and the resemblance does not seem to be fortuitous. Evidently Ledoux conceived of the *barrières* as a kind of experimental laboratory of typologies and their possible trans-

The Barrières of Paris.
Vignettes from Plate 10
of "The buildings of
the city of Paris,"
engraved by Gaitte.

formations, dissociated from their previous uses and open to new ones. For the formal themes of these gates re-appeared in many of the projects for Chaux: in the triumphal arches of his double houses for fashion merchants that echoed those of the Barrière Poissonnière; in the barrel-vaults of the house of the river surveyors that were taken from the Barrière de la Santé; or in the country house for a stock broker with its cylindrical form like that of Saint-Martin. Similarly, motifs like the rustication of the Barrière Sainte-Marie re-appeared as the artificial "logs" used for the different rustic ateliers of the forest; the amphiprostyle temple of the Barrière de la Glacière was borrowed entirely for the country house depicted in Plate 22 of *L'Architecture*.

More immediately the "museum" of types formed by the *barrières* was seen by Ledoux to have a didactic role similar to that proposed by Louis-François Cassas for his museum of architectural models at roughly the same time.[10] Full-scale "models" of antique precedents, demonstrations of their adaptation to modern uses, the *barrières*, like all the ideal projects published in *L'Architecture*, were object lessons for architect and citizen. There the architectural student would be able to study a series of "compositions as varied as they are numerous," [6] paradigms of combination and characterisation; the inhabitants of Paris would, for their part, easily recognise the emblems of "public virtues assembled in a circle to level the public mind," "constructions whose diversity slakes the thirst of desire." [18] Ledoux's urban aesthetic was evidently panoramic and theatrical, projecting on the scale of the city itself the three-hundred-and-sixty-degree vision of the new institutions of illusion, the panoramas themselves. In this sense, the "transformational grammar" of the *barrières* was calculated, following the precepts of Locke and Condillac, to form a literal "chain of association" stimulating the perception of an urban *flâneur* beating the bounds of the city along the new boulevards; as if one barrière were to be de-composing into the next, only to be re-composed into another variation.

Ledoux's double aim of aesthetic and moral embellishment was perhaps most strongly exemplified in the designs for eight huge taverns, prepared as an integral part of the urban programme of the *barrières* at the behest of Calonne. These "guinguettes," projected to replace the popular resorts of the *banlieue* that had grown up outside the walls to escape the city wine-tax, had, in Calonne's mind, the purpose not only of recuperating lost revenues on the sale of wine for the profit of the state, but also to police and control a crowd that, despite the obviously recreational function of the *guinguettes*, was a threat to social order: new state-run taverns would act to neutralise the dangers of riot, sedition or simple brigandage at the same time as palliating the lot of the poor.[11] In Ledoux's paternalistic words, "the people" would here be able "to efface the memory of your hardships through the games that will be prepared for you, in the festivals of which you will be the object; to drink away your fatigue to oblivion, and, in restorative relaxation, you will draw new strengths and the courage needed for your labours." [6] To this end, Ledoux invented a new building-type – the ancestor of the *café concert* of the nineteenth century – based on the activities common in existing *guinguettes*. With public salons, long galleries for eating and drinking, courtyards for dancing surrounded by arcades, these inns were planned in variations of the square and Greek cross plans (save one which was triangular, enclosed in a circle). At the centre of many were separate pavilions, recalling the *barrières* modelled on the Villa Rotunda. They were each conceived with specific sites in mind, quarters where places of popular resort were already to be found: the Faubourgs Poissonnière, du Temple, Saint-Antoine, Saint-Marceau, Vaugirard and Chaillot, and the rue Menilmontant and the Quai de la Rapée. This last was planned as a riverside tavern, its courtyards replaced by pools for swimming and boating.

Perhaps as his most daring design among these institutions for popular recreation, Ledoux conceived a huge "Pleasure House," [Maison de Plaisir] for the hill of Montmartre, the function

Perspective view,
plan and section
of the guinguette
Saint-Marceau. From:
L'Architecture...,
Ramée edition, Plate 231.

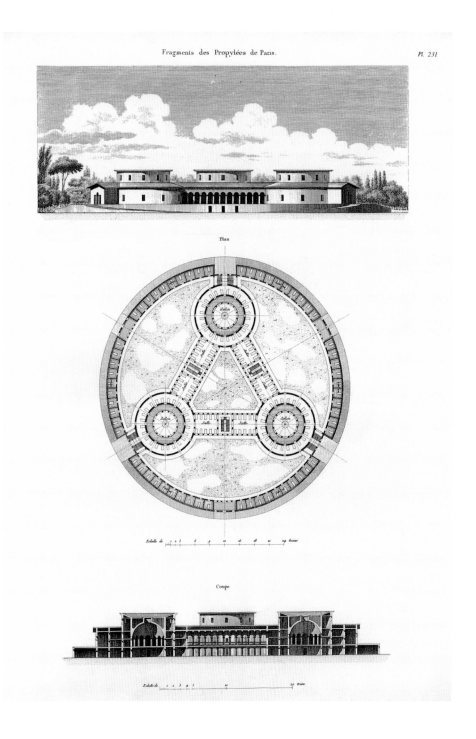

of which was revealed wittily in the intrusion of a phallic-shaped temple into its circular enclosure. In section, this licensed house of prostitution seemed to take up the entire hill, sculpted into the shape of a huge cylinder, with long stairs and ramps leading up to the monument itself, as if to mimic on a public scale the routes of erotic initiation so popular in libertine gatherings and *contes érotiques*. "For the first time, " Ledoux concluded, "you will see on the same scale the magnificence of the *guinguette* and of the palace." [18] Completing this roster of "people's houses," was a design for a "Popular Monument," a recreational pavilion, like the *guinguettes*, but conceived in a "popular" style of architecture, with projecting pantile roofs, half-timbered brick walls, resembling a country farmhouse. [Ramée, II, pls. 234-35] Such institutions were, for Ledoux and his protectors in the final years before the Revolution, a last attempt to apply the environmental and social precepts of the Enlightenment on behalf of public order and in the formation of a pacified and moralised underclass, healthy enough to work and happy enough to be content. In this context, the much later formulation by Le Corbusier of the blunt choice between architecture and revolution already seems ingenuous.

10. PHYSIOCRATIC REGIONALISM

"I had travelled for two years for my education, when I heard, at Lyons, that the government had opened up considerable public works in a part of Franche-Comté. This province offers a vast field for natural history, commerce and industry." [43]

The Saline de Chaux, while planned in response to a specific programme, was clearly conceived in the I770s within a general policy of opening up the eastern provinces of France to trade and commerce and stimulating a renewal of their agriculture. Annexed to France only a century before, Franche-Comté, with its independent population, parliament, and customs, was both strategically and economically important, not least against the increasing power of the Genevan republic and the Swiss cantons. Trudaine the elder, with the help of Perronet and his corps of engineers, had begun to plan an expanded highway and canal network, and the policy was continued by his son Trudaine de Montigny with the support of Turgot. Later, Calonne would actively support the development of new industries to supplement the already growing iron and glass production of the region.[1] Jean Querret, the chief engineer of the province, proposed a renewal of the canals, and his project was expanded by another engineer, Philippe Bertrand, in the 1770s, who projected a canal joining the Doubs to the Saône, and thence through Alsace to the Rhine;[2] a project that he

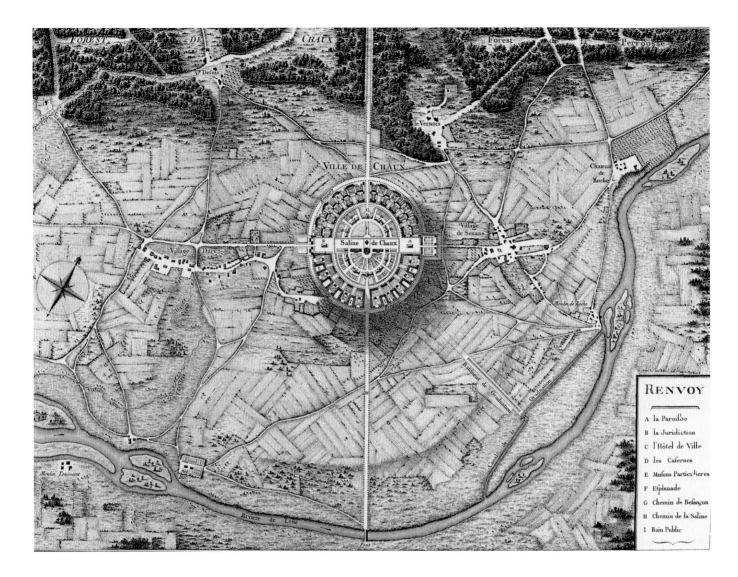

conceived would, with the addition of the Canal de Bourgogne already started, form a network to make Franche-Comté "the centre of commerce between the three seas, and make of it the most magnificent establishment."[3] In this context, Ledoux's claim that he had from the outset envisaged the Saline de Chaux as the industrial nucleus of a government-sponsored new town, a centre for regional development seems entirely credible. While it is far from clear that the designs for the temples, public baths, markets, houses of commerce and games that he mentioned in this connection were themselves more than ideas

in the 1770s, it is certain that Ledoux, as he stated, presented "the projects for a town with the growth to which it is susceptible." Cellerier speaks of this town as being presented to Turgot – that is before 1776 – and Ledoux's hopes, if not Turgot's reception of them, were no doubt supported by two other new towns proposed for the same region: that of Versoix, a project with which Choiseul intended to combat the economic power of Geneva and wich had attracted the notice of Voltaire and the designing skills of Querret between 1766 and 1777; and that of Carouge, founded by Victor-Emmanuel of Sardinia for the

same reasons between 1772 and 1792.[4] Ledoux, indeed, made his expectations explicit in a note to the prospectus to *L'Architecture*, where, speaking of the "Ville de Chaux," he added, "The project for building Versoix has been abandoned, the Duke de Choiseul having left the ministry." [*Prospectus*, 9] Ledoux might have hoped that Trudaine, in turning down Querret's request to restart work at Versoix, would be the more receptive to his project for Chaux.

That the land for an expansion of the Saline was already envisaged by the administration is shown by the surveyor's "Plan de la forêt de Chaux, de

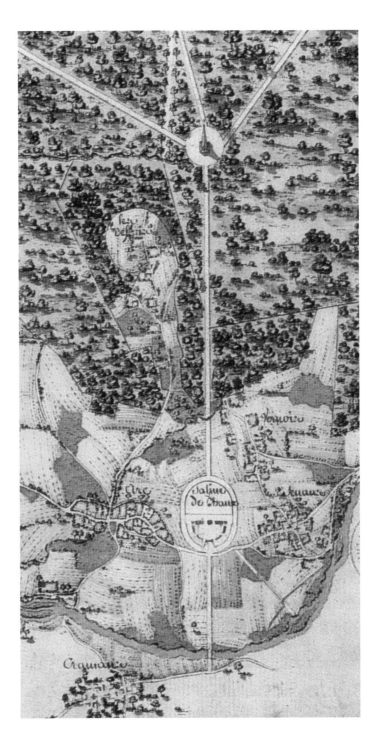

l'emplacement de la saline, du bâtiment de graduation, du canal et des routes projettées dans
cette forêt pour le service de la saline," a map
of the entire forest drawn in the late 1770s to plot
the routes for the provision of fuel for the Saline.[5]
Here, already, the semi-circle of the Saline is doubled with an oval surrounding boulevard in order
to delineate the site for expansion into a town.
Additionally, the north-south axis of the plan,
from the bridge over the River Loue and beyond
into the forest, terminates in a giant obelisk at
the centre of the radiating forest routes, which
in turn, and a little later, were to be marked with
free-standing Doric columns at their intersec-
tions: the first stage in endowing the forest and
its inhabitants with an architecture of control.

This map obviously provided the basis for the
more imaginative elaboration by the engraver
Dupuis, entitled "Carte des environs de la Saline
de Chaux" [*L'Architecture* Plate 14]; it details
the town envisaged by Ledoux. Its plan is com-
pact and enclosed within an oval formed by the
doubling of the Saline: this is shown as built,
and still surrounded by its wall. The semi-circle
of buildings to the north exactly mirror the form
of those of the Saline, similarly enclosed by a wall,
and describe a military barracks and a town hall,
underlying the fortified and strategic nature of
this border settlement. Outside the double walls
of the barracks and Saline, to east and west on
the cross axis of the oval, are two public build-

Perspective view
of the bridge
over the River Loue.
From: *L'Architecture...*,
Ramée edition,
Plate 109.

ings, a parish church and law courts; other institutions, such as the public baths, are indicated only by letter. Around the central oval runs a tree-lined boulevard that provides an exterior circulation for a town whose centre is, so to speak, inaccessible. This ring road services the private housing, planned in reticulated terraces around courtyards and gardens, their patterns differing for reasons of orientation, from north to south. These terraces, their geometries reminiscent of the crescents and rows of George Dance and John Wood in England, are themselves enclosed by a peripheral boulevard, designated, appropriately enough, "a rampart." Two roads lead north and south, to the forest of Chaux and the River Loue respectively; for the rest, the landscape of the region, its houses, water mills, ferry, chateaux, villages and foresters' hamlets were left unchanged, as were the canal and graduation building of the Saline. As Wolfgang Herrmann has shown, this engraving was no doubt prepared in two stages, the first simply to show the Saline in its context, as the title indicates, the second to represent the town planned sometime afterwards.

A second version of Ledoux's ideas for the Ville de Chaux, depicted in the "Vue perspective de la Ville de Chaux" [*L'Architecture* Plate 15], reveals a very different conception of the town however. The closed, geometric and fortified character, appropriate to a garrison, is replaced by an open picturesque distribution that reflected the new interest in landscape design of the 1780s. The central oval of the barracks and the Saline is still in place, but the enclosing wall is obscured by the clouds of smoke that pour from the factory windows, and the parade ground is filled with assembled troops. To the east, replacing the small parish church of the earlier scheme, is Ledoux's developed design for the church of Chaux, with its domed rotunda and four porches recalling at once the Pantheon and Palladio. The law courts have been replaced by a first project for the market, similar to the rotunda of Saint-Martin or the Halle au Blé of Le Camus de Mézières. To the rear are visible the public baths and what seems to be a first project for the stock exchange. Schools, monasteries and farms mingle old and new construction; parish churches,

individual houses, one like that planned for the Chevalier de Mannery of Salins, dot the landscape, taking the place of the regular terraces of the first plan. The aesthetic is that of the Abbé Delille's popular evocation of the art of gardens, *Les Jardins*, of 1782. The dating of this perspective is helped by the institutions depicted: the engraver, Pierre-Gabriel Berthault, also drew the perspective of the public baths and the graduation building of the Saline, while the church, engraved by Sellier, was another early project. The ensemble was evidently designed between 1780 and 1784 when, under the inspiration of the Académie's programme for the Prix d'Émulation, Ledoux redesigned the market with a scheme close to that of La Clothe, the winner of 1783.[6] These pre-Revolutionary plans for Chaux were described by Ledoux in terms that suggest his debt to the developed Physiocracy of Trudaine and Turgot: one that extended the rigorous division between sterile and productive activities insisted on by the founders of the doctrine, du Quesnay and Mirabeau, to embrace a more liberal view of the place of industry and commerce

Right:
Bridge over the
River Loue, section
and plan of the
foundations. From:
L'Architecture..., Plate 3.

Below:
Bridge
over the River Loue,
detail of model.
Arc-et-Senans,
Musée Ledoux.

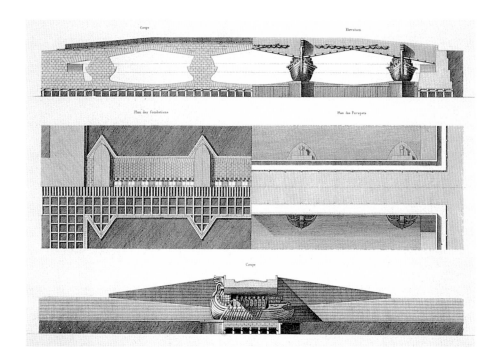

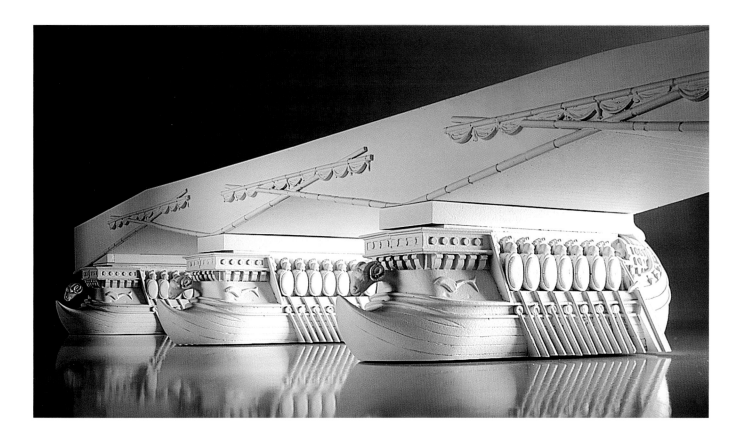

in the circle of the economy.[7] Ledoux himself made much of the image of the circle, an image that tied together the economic cycle, the natural unfolding of the seasons, and his architectural forms; he compared the oval plan of the town to the "elliptical" course of the sun, and found in the circular city, as he had in the circular theatre, a principle of natural form: "Everything is circular in nature." [223] Even as in the antique fable the Milky Way was sprung from a drop of milk falling from Juno's breast, so in Chaux, Ledoux's town was, he claimed, spawned by a drop of falling water, source of irrigation and of brine. For Ledoux, this natural intersection of source and product, expressed so dramatically in the overturned urns in the facade of the Saline, was equally mirrored in the form of the town, which on the "Carte des environs de la saline de Chaux" is carefully shaded so as to resemble such a drop of water.

Sustaining this economic foundation, Ledoux's repertory of institutions also held Physiocratic overtones: the public baths, using the salt water, as at Salins, as a natural therapy for the inhabitants (Ledoux, in prison under the Terror, was later to offer these "clinics" to the French armies as the price of his release); the markets, a centre of agricultural distribution and a source of charity and instruction of the poor. Only hospitals and prisons are lacking, their absence explained, following the Physiocrats Nicolas Baudeau and

Dupont de Nemours, by the salubrious effect of the natural surroundings on a population rendered happy, healthy, and honest. The stock exchange, finally, would be no longer a centre for corrupt speculation, the ruinous activities of John Law, but returned to a natural function of regulation and encouragement of trade and commerce, distributing its profits for the benefit of the needy.

Later, in the 1780s, under the influence of Calonne, and with the example of the foundries, blast furnaces, and glass works being installed to the south-west at Le Creusot, Ledoux supplemented these charitable and agrarian institutions with the design of a large cannon foundry to supply the armies of the East.[8] Four giant blast furnaces, pyramidal in shape, stand at the corners of the factory; along the sides are workshops for carpentry, joinery, chasing, casting, locksmiths, cartwrights, and smiths, arranged as if drawn from the textbook examples of Diderot's *Encyclopédie*. At the centre, the forges themselves are housed in higher sheds intersecting at the director's building. A canal and subsidiary basins provide water throughout the works. Clustered around this factory, depicted in Bovinet's perspective view, Ledoux envisaged a veritable *cité industrielle*, with houses for merchants, artists, cabinet makers, wholesalers, and artisans of all kinds – Ledoux's idealised extension of what on the "Carte des environs de la saline de Chaux" was marked simply as the Moulin de Roche.

Evoking the results he expected from such industrial and commercial development, Ledoux paraphrased almost to the letter the reports of the canal and road engineers of the Ponts et Chaussées as they had argued for a new canal network; he imagined Chaux becoming the centre of a huge network of trade: "The line of the major [north-south] axis crosses the River Loue, immense plains, the town, the forest, the River Doubs, the Geneva canal, the Swiss pastures; to the left, the Meuse, the Moselle, the Rhine, the

port of Antwerp, the North Sea carrying to the Siberian deserts early fruits and so many desires for our commerce and arts ... The smaller [east-west] axis aligns the roads between Arc and Senans, the forges of Roche, paper mills, saw mills. What movement! Some polish the steel, chase the brass, blow the glass; others cast the white hot metal that sustains the rights of nations." [72] In the last years of the eighteenth century, with the completion of the Canal du Centre by the engineer Emiliand Gauthey, the open-

ing of the route from the Loire to the Saône and the extension of the Canal du Languedoc, such a dream was less utopian than it was an application of common engineering wisdom joined to Turgot's doctrine of progress.

Above:
City of Chaux,
perspective view
of the public baths.
From: *L'Architecture...*,
Plate 82.

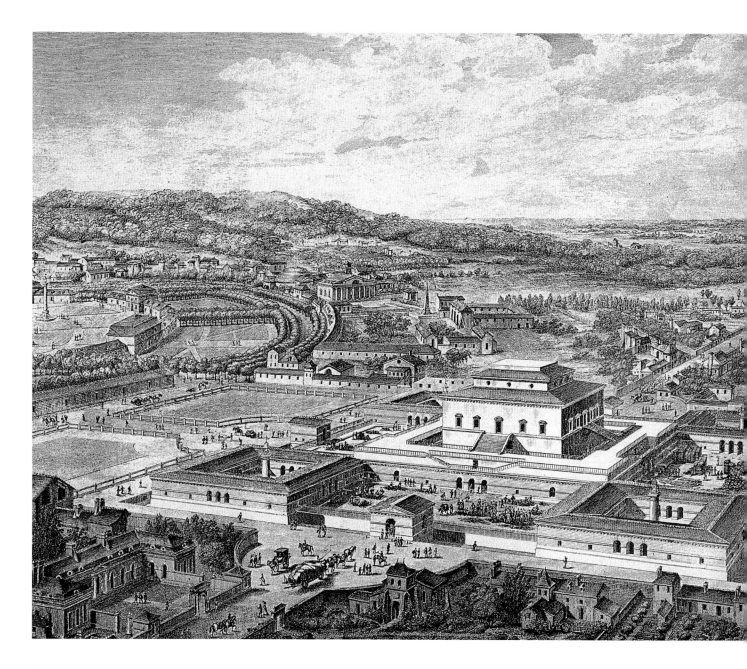

Left:
City of Chaux,
perspective view
of the market.
From: *L'Architecture...*,
Plate 79.

Right:
City of Chaux,
plan of the market.
From: *L'Architecture...*,
Plate 76.

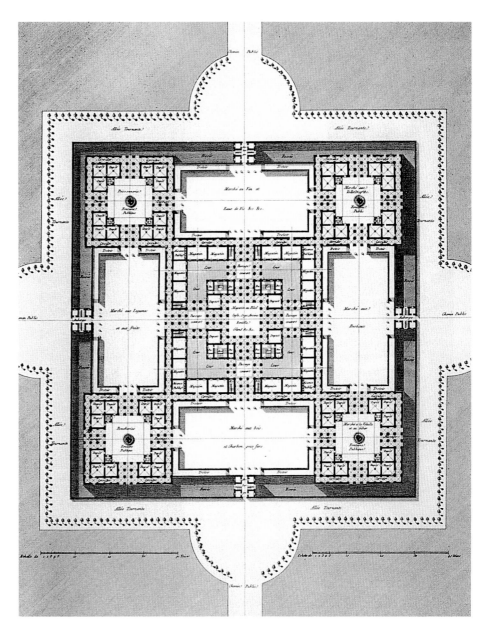

AGRONOMY

11. AGRONOMIC ARCHITECTURE

"If you send back to cultivate the precious earth those ungrateful souls who have belittled it despite the fact that it has showered them with its riches – how many powerful levers to overcome inaction and motivate industry, how many outlets opened for the economy!" [74]

If the theoretical models of the Physiocrats and their followers provided the diagrammatic forms and spatial extensions for Ledoux's "circular" idealisation of Chaux, it was the practical proposals of the agronomists that gave him the programmes for his rural architecture in the 1780s and 1790s.[1] While the economists confined their speculation to the *shape* of systems, the agronomists, self-appointed reformers of agriculture and rural customs, were concerned with what they considered *practical* and useful knowledge. Where the Physiocrat was a philosopher of principle, the *agronome* was empirical and didactic. Following the example of the English, many of Ledoux's patrons and friends investigated new methods of crop rotation, breeding, implements, drainage and enclosures; Buffon at the Jardin du Roi and on his estate at Montbard collaborated with Trudaine de Montigny, who in turn founded a model sheepfold on his own estate; Turgot experimented in the Berry; Malesherbes, a botanical enthusiast, studied arboriculture; Montesquiou, like many others, proposed to establish a model village at Maupertuis, replacing the old

Left side:
House of the
agricultural guards
of Maupertuis,
perspective view,
elevation and section.
From: *L'Architecture...*,
Ramée edition,
Plate 254.

Above:
Barrel-makers'
workshop.
From: *L'Architecture...*,
Plate 88.

Below:
House of the
agricultural guards,
plan. From:
L'Architecture ...,
Ramée edition,
Plate 254.

Right page:
House
of the directors
of the Loue,
perspective view.
From: *L'Architecture*...,
Plate 6.

one partly destroyed with the expansion of the garden, for his peasant farmers. At the centre of this circle was the Abbé Delille, giving antique authority and contemporary aesthetic expression to the briefly fashionable "back-to-the-land" movement, a belated critique of the absenteeism that had allowed so many rural properties to decline as landlords gathered at the court of Versailles or in the city. Ledoux, with his early experience in building rural *fabriques* for the Eaux et Forêts and stables and outhouses for Montesquiou and Madame du Barry, as well as for the Saline, was well versed in the rules for proper ventilation, drainage and construction; indeed the text of *L'Architecture* at times reads like a com-

pilation of antique and modern maxims for sound agricultural practice distilled from Pliny and Varro, Pierre Vannière and the Abbé Rozier. Just before the Revolution he drew up schemes for a *ferme parée* or model farm and a sheepfold for the estate of Louis de Boisgelin at La Roche Bernard in Normandy and for a proposed École Rurale at Meilhan, Berry, for the Duc de Béthune-Charost.[2] All took account of the latest wisdom, applying the admonition of the reformers at a grand and expansive scale in order to produce a repertory of types for the exploitation of the countryside as varied and comprehensive as those he had designed for the city.

This productive vision was not confined, however,

to the large-scale land reform projects of the *seigniors*; Ledoux was equally interested in the life and needs of the small tenant farmer, designing a modest barn or *grange parée* to be supervised by a "petit économe," as well as for a service court, porticoes for grain storage, and a horse trough and watering place for the villagers of Chaux. Adopting traditional layouts, with accomodation for animals and storage on the ground floor, and rooms for the farmer, his family and servants on the upper floors, Ledoux transformed them into architectural versions or rural types, with provision for ventilation and hygienic drainage, applying motifs taken from Palladio and the Tuscan vernacular. Ledoux's most polemical campaign, following the English agricultural reformers, was waged against the *chaumières* or thatched hovels of the rural poor: "to destroy the thatched cottages is to return man to his dignity, his security." [103] Like François Cointereaux, whose patent method of construction out of hardened earth, or *pisé*, had not yet been demonstrated a failure, Ledoux designed a series of plans for simple houses based on his estimate of the essential needs (*les besoins*) of a single family.[3] Here, he referred back to that discourse of origins current in the first half of the century; but, rather than proposing some abstract and elementary model of structure like the Abbé Laugier, he preferred to return architecture to its social roots. For Ledoux, "origins" were to be found in

the primitive geometries that sheltered typical activities, joined to principles of sound construction economically applied. Laugier had presented an optimistic image of a self-sufficient "natural man" building his own shelter out of the trees of the forest and thereby inventing the aesthetic system for all subsequent classical architecture. Ledoux, anticipating what later critics, from Goethe to Durand, would point out, that Laugier's open, four-posted hut was a poor shelter at best, reversed the narrative dramatically. In a critical image of his *L'Architecture*, he depicted "L'abri du pauvre" [Pl. 33] ironically enough as a single, stunted tree growing out of a stony islet set in an infinite and forbidding sea; beneath this "shelter" sits a naked and shivering pauper on a few rough stones, holding his hands out in supplication to the skies where, atop a bank of clouds that disperses the rays of the sun toward the earth – the first rays of the Enlightenment – the gods of Olympus and the muses

of the arts and sciences are assembled, ready to dispense their munificence. "The Architect is there," wrote Ledoux, "surrounded by clouds." [195] Clearly the architect should be ready to step in, where increasing specialisation had removed the path of self-help from the poor.

Some time after 1784, apparently contemporary with his designs for the *barrières*, Ledoux planned a model village for the estate of Montesquiou at Maupertuis which brought together these concerns in a single perspective view.[4] A collection of variations on his first plan for a Maison de Commis stood along two streets intersecting at right angles at the centre: each with different roof formations and massing, with their own fenced plots containing orchards, arbours, kitchen gardens and vegetable patches, the front onto the main street and back onto the village common lands. In the foreground, a figure that could have been taken from the *Encyclopédie* or the Abbé Rozier's treatise on agriculture ploughs the fields.

At the centre of the village Ledoux places the "village church," but now transformed into a huge primitive temple, peripteral, with a square Tuscan order, standing on a two-sided pyramid of stairs that invades the structure vertically as it rises to the central altar. A procession of villagers, celebrating an important moment in the life of the commune, is shown wending its way to this dominating focus of religious and secular order. What, otherwise, might remind us of Rousseau's happy vision of the mountain villages around Neufchâtel takes on, in Ledoux's paternalist version, the aspect of a community bound by agricultural pursuits and a respect for primitive natural religion in a hierarchy that is topped by the landowner himself, Deist and freemasonic master of ceremonies.

Completing his roster of rural dwellings, Ledoux, again in the 1780s, designed a set of *fabriques* for artisans more directly connected with the external economy of the Saline de Chaux and

L'Abri du Pauvre,
the Poor Man's Shelter.
From: *L'Architecture* ...,
Plate 33.

its forest. The omnivorous demand for cordwood, construction timber, charcoal, iron, casks and barrels was the occasion to imagine workshops and collective housing for all the metiers of the forest: woodcutters, sawyers, coopers, carpenters, charcoal-burners together with their overseers, the forest guards and river surveyors.[5] Isolated from each other, set in clearings that were joined by a network of *allées*, these small pavilions were each given an architectural char-

the effect of confirming the domination of the factory over its region while reforming the life and morals of their undoubtedly rough inhabitants, who lived, according to one contemporary observer, much like wolves in the forest, running half-naked and hardly sheltered by branches and leaves. Inside Ledoux's replacements for these real primitive huts, the material conditions for happiness were, as in the workers' buildings in the Saline, given spatial form. All were planned round a common fireplace, with bedrooms and workshops deployed around a central double-height space, implying the formation of community if not the stimulation of fraternity.[6] Outside, built of unfashioned timber or its imitation, their forms were emblematic of their rustic role; domed, as in the dwelling of the charcoal-burner, or pyramidally roofed, as in his workshop. On one level, these huts might be read as the primitive versions of the bourgeois lodges; Ledoux was well aware of the deep-rooted associational life of the forest *compagnonnage*, or brotherhoods, and perhaps wished to reproduce such natural forms of community in architecture. On another level, and especially in three of the *fabriques* – the house for the coopers, the house for the river surveyors and the house for the agricultural guards of Maupertuis – Ledoux was evidently seeking to "speak to the people" in a characteristic and unambiguous sign language particularly appropriate to an illiterate population raised on the hieroglyph-

ic bibles and calendars of the *bibliothèque bleue*.[7] Thus, in architectural "emblems" that almost caricature their subject matter, the coopers are housed in a structure formed out of two intersecting cylinders, grooved to resemble barrels; the river surveyors dwell in a pipe-like house through which the river, object of their surveillance, flows like a waterfall as they exercise their visual oversight on a bridge beneath that also functions as a billiard room; the agricultural guards are endowed with a shelter in the shape of a complete sphere, symbolising their guardianship of the flocks. This latter conceit is represented in a perspective that demonstrates Ledoux's mediating iconography: the sphere of the new house stands at the apex of a triangle formed by the old rustic hut of branches and leaves to the left, and the rising sun in the background, a triangle that confirms the masonic origins of the image.

acter of their own, envisaged, so to speak, as "figures" of production, dramatising by their primitive orders and geometrical rhetoric rural occupations already dignified by Diderot and his collaborators. In Ledoux's mind they would have

Panarèthéeon.

Vue Perspective.

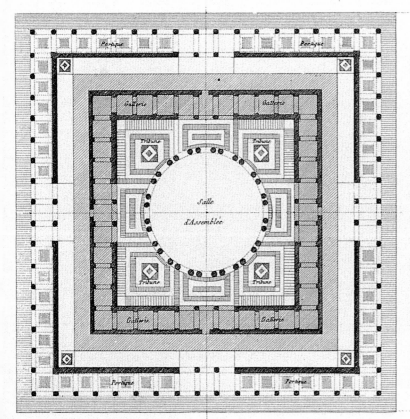

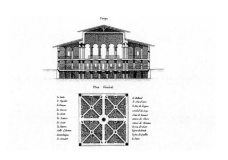

12. TEMPLES OF SOCIABILITY

Left page:
Perspective view
and plans of the
Panaréthéon.
From: *L'Architecture*...,
Plate 92.

Above:
Section and general plan
of the monument
for recreational purposes.
From: *L'Architecture*...,
Plate 83.

"One can be made virtuous or vicious, like the rough or polished stone, from the friction of our surroundings; happiness and well-being can thus be found in the attractive feeling of common pleasures." [3]

The idea of a space that would construct and reform social mores by its form and symbolic representation was, in the late eighteenth century, deeply embedded in the theory and practice of bourgeois and aristocratic sociability, and especially of freemasonry. In the last thirty years of the century, following the consolidation of the order under the aegis of the Grand Orient in 1773, the lodge as a type, both as built and as metaphor, emerged as the paradigm of sociable space, the space of happiness achieved through brotherhood.[1] Its layout was calculated to inform and structure rituals of initiation and festivity; its architectural references, drawn from the old charges of operative masonry, and the idea of the original Temple, were symbolic of building a new social "edifice;" its membership included many *philosophes* and professionals who took their Deist and reformist ideology entirely seriously; its influence between the 1770s and 1789, extending to an estimated affiliation of over ten thousand in the Grand Orient lodges alone, not counting the schismatic Grand Lodge and hundreds of quasi-masonic sects, touched every level of society, lending its dis-

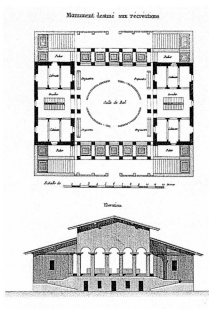

Monument destiné aux récreations

Elevation

Plan du Premier Etage

Coupe

Plan Général.

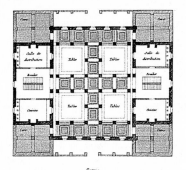

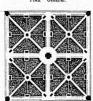

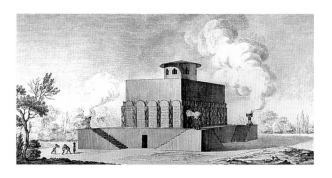

Right page:
Perspective view
of the Oikéma.
From: *L'Architecture*...,
Plate 103.

Left, top to bottom:
General plan
of the monument for
recreational purposes.
From: *L'Architecture*...,
Plate 83.

Pespective view
of the Pacifère.
From: *L'Architecture*...,
Plate 40.

course and symbolism to the generalised utopianism of the epoch.[2]

For the architect, whose own tradition had been pillaged for the lodge's eclectic iconography, membership took on added significance that supplemented the obvious opportunities for patronage in these mixed circles. Not only would the masonic architect have the responsibility to design the lodge itself – Pierre Poncet, Charles de Wailly and Ledoux's student Sobre were among those who contributed to masonic architecture properly speaking – but he might draw on the forms of ritual and the symbols of brotherhood for the representation of institutional and social projects. Thus, in the work of those who were known to be inscribed masons like de Wailly, Brongniart, Le Camus de Mézières, Chalgrin, Vaudoyer and Cellerier, as well as in that of those whose formal affiliation was less clear, like Boullée and Ledoux, the imagery of masonry is prolifically employed, either as decoration, or, in the case of de Wailly, Boullée and Ledoux, in the serious embodiment of ideals.

Ledoux's poetics of sociability, in particular, cannot be explained, either in its primitive geometries or in its ritually symbolic forms, without reference to this ubiquitous movement. Ledoux, familiar with the ambiance of the orthodox lodges through his patrons and friends, was also, according to the testimony of the English writer, William Beckford, affiliated to a more unorthodox lodge on the outskirts of Paris in 1784 – the year of his most daring experiments in primary forms. In a long and perhaps over-dramatised letter, the young pre-Romantic novelist described visiting this site in the company of Ledoux, ostensibly to view an allegorically decorated ceiling the design of which Beckford had seen in Ledoux's office.[3] The architecture of the lodge itself, with its initiatory sequence of spaces, moving in a kind of architectural historical order from primitive pyramidal wood piles, through medieval halls, eighteenth-century cottages, to a salon containing a mesmerist basin, and finally to the "chapel," lit by a single ray of light, was, Beckford implied, designed by Ledoux. The setting of this "lodge" in a deserted landscape surrounded by a high wall resembled that of many lodges of the epoch, and especially the celebrated lodge of the Eveillés. Beckford also implies a connection, entirely reasonable given Ledoux's circle, with the entourage of the Duc d'Orléans. Certainly from the mid-1780s on, Ledoux drew on freemasonic imagery increasingly for his idealised designs for *fabriques*, and by the time of the Revolution he was incorporating the symbols, rituals and even an idealised "type" of the lodge in the utopian institutions of the city of Chaux. Indeed, in one sense, this utopia, described in *L'Architecture*, dedicated to the realisation of social happiness, joined by bonds of brotherhood and confirmed by the architecture of its monuments, may be read

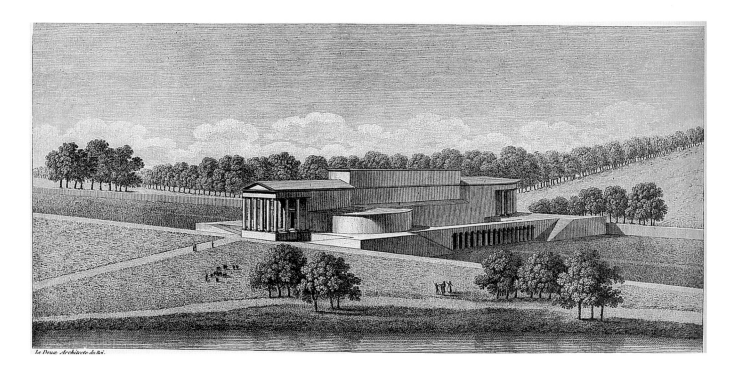

Le Deux Architecte du Roi.

as the natural extension of masonic ideals into a grand design for social reform. While, under the Revolution, the Grand Orient dissolved itself in support of a generalised Republican "brotherhood," Ledoux, forced into isolation, turned to a more private vision of brotherhood as the source of an architecture not yet invented. In the landscape garden-like setting of the forest of Chaux and the plain of the River Loue, he imagined a series of ideal lodges, each dedicated functionally and symbolically to a particular social virtue.

First was the Pacifère, an acknowledged neologism ("pacifère" or the conciliator," noted Ledoux, "one says "morbifère," "somnifère," "mortifère," thus one can say "pacifère,"[113]) and therefore in the tradition of institutions invented by means of language such as Rétif de la Bretonne's "Parthénion" or, later, Fourier's "Phalanstère." This monument stood, in Ledoux's city, for the law, for justice; but, in what he saw as "the new-born town" there would be little need for traditional prisons or courts of law: Chaux "will perhaps be inhabited by less criminal men, over

whom reason and their self-interest will have some influence." [114] Mediation would take the place of imprisonment in this building of symbolic form, where, raised on a podium, the public hall leads to a square audience chamber lit from above by a circular lantern. Ledoux explained, "The form of a cube is the symbol of Justice, one represents it sitting on a square stone, prescribing punishments for vice and rewards for virtue." [115] On the outer walls mosaic tablets are inscribed with the principles of the new justice, the maxims of morality, framed by a giant order in the shape of the Roman fasces, symbol of unity. The central tablet to each end of the rectangular chamber acts as the door, giving the effect, when closed, of a hermetically sealed vault; at each corner burn eternal flames on tripods. To the left of the building Ledoux depicts what obviously is a scene of reconciliation – two wrestlers supervised by guards resolving their dispute. Less temple-like in plan, but literally cubic, is the Maison d'Union, dedicated to universal brotherhood, a natural principle, necessary, Ledoux states, for the sustenance of order.

On the walls of the cube, lit from the top by a cylindrical light, are inscribed maxims, as if taken from Marmontel, eulogising union and its benefits. Reinforcing its primary school quality, this institution will offer all the facilities of a "popular university" supported by contributions from the Ferme Générale (a tax of one sou on every cake of salt).

Complementing the houses of Peace and Union is a third, carrying the neologism of "Panarèthéon" or "accomplished virtue." A pure cube, raised up on two stories of ramps and arcades, it encloses a cylindrical assembly room, again lit from above. It is conceived as an iconographical school of virtue, "a school of morals where the lessons teach of the duties of man."[180] Here the cube is a "symbol of immutability," surrounding the gathered inhabitants who in turn surround their didactic philosopher at the centre. The ramps symbolise so many degrees of perfection, leading to the highest room as if in some masonic rite. On the walls are carved allegories of form and beauty – the Graces, the Days, the Hours, Wisdom in the guise of Minerva, the Canon

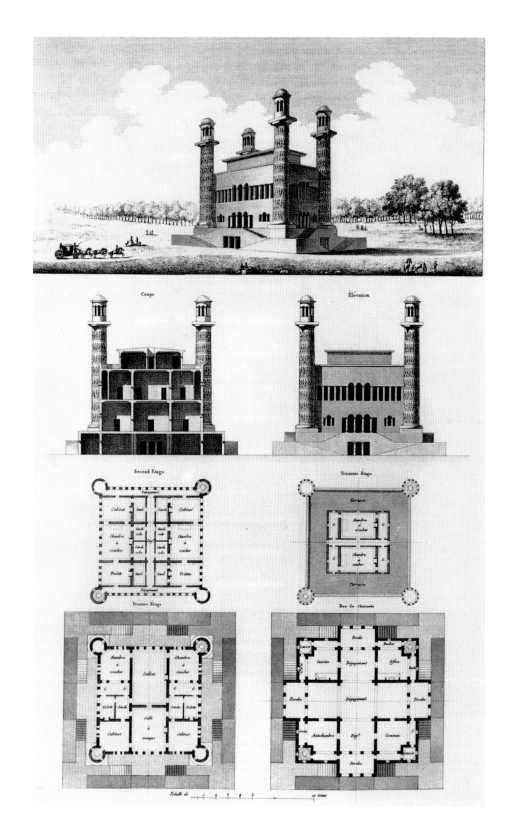

of Polyclitus, together with the troupe of social virtues, seemingly carved according to the precepts of Winckelmann – a veritable museum of characteristics or neo-classical memory theatre, prefiguring the more historicist pantheons of the early nineteenth century, private and public, from Canova to Schinkel.

A fourth institution, the Temple of Memory, confirms the association of Ledoux's symbolic monuments to a revived art of memory. Its function is displayed by four monumental Trajan columns attached to each corner, topped, like those of Fischer von Erlach's Karlskirche in Vienna, with oriental minarets, thereby reinforcing the hallucinatory world of Chaux which like some *conte orientale* from Crebillon or Diderot is suspended halfway between East and West. Wrapping these columns are bas-reliefs recounting the exploits of women, heroines private and public, sustainers and teachers of morals to the young. The dedication of this lodge "of adoption" to women is intended to balance the stern male

qualities of the other lodges.[4] It was also to be, Ledoux opined, the favoured burial place of its architect, who dreamt of finding his resting place surrounded by the tender attentions of those who delighted him in life.

Other freemasonic symbols may be detected in Ledoux's ideal city, from the fallen columns and three dancing children in the engraving of the House of Education to the more overtly libertine rites of passage suggested in the phallic plan of the Oikéma. But even as Ledoux avoided a strict allegiance to historical quotation in the assembly of his urban typologies, so in the imaginary institutions of Chaux, he steers away from the eclectic and literal citation of freemasonic paraphernalia, preferring to absorb all references once more in the comforting abstraction of pure geometry. Ledoux's "système symbolique," at once returns architecture to universals and allows it to participate in a history-free world, one where the keys to signification reside less in a precise iconographical or stylistic source – the

art-historians' pleasure – than in the communication of a precise transformation in a chain of such transformations. These are evident in plan – the nine-square grid of Palladio given apparently endless permutations, or the triple-square rectangle of the typical lodge. In this sense, Ledoux, as Emil Kaufmann pointed out, may be seen as the true progenitor of Durand and Dubut, but with an important difference. Ledoux's transformations are never gratuitous, never divorced from the need to signify; nor are they coded and systematised in elevation, section and plan. Each, whether for a public or private function, is carefully calibrated to its supposed use by means of a representative code based on the meaning of spatial order, vertical and horizontal, lit or unlit, central or peripheral; if, after this, the addition of architectural motifs and attributes might enhance the "reading" of the building, Ledoux will carefully select one or two, directly contrasting with the plain surfaces that reveal the inner form, simply for effect. The perfection of

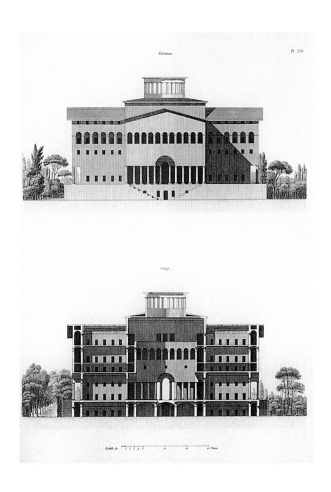

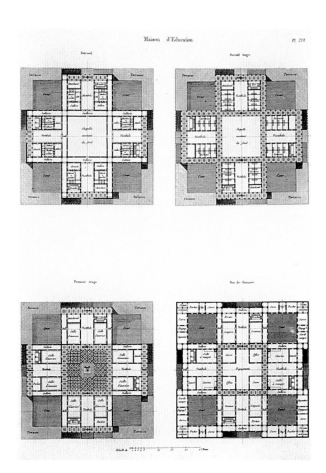

Above left:
Elevation and
section of a house
of education.
From: *L'Architecture*...,
Plate 106.

Above right:
Mezzanine, ground,
first and second floor
plans of a house
of education.
From: *L'Architecture*...,
Plate 105.

Right page:
Perspective view
of a house of education.
From: *L'Architecture*...,
Plate 107.

a work, in fact, resides in the extent to which a volumetric interior and a massing of the exterior might become indissolubly both meaning in themselves and a symbol of that meaning.

Hence the privilege Ledoux accords to the cemetery. A half-buried sphere, built into the quarry excavated for building the city, it stands at the centre of three tiers of catacombs, planned radially, like a perfect ideal town. Its void is impenetrable, save perhaps by the spirits of the dead, provided as in life, with a communal meeting place. From the outside, the dome is smooth, as if carved from the natural rock rising above the flat and deserted site; inside, lit only by a circular opening at its summit, it, in Ledoux's words, presents only "the image of nothingness". [195] The allegorical inter-text of this monument is provided in Ledoux's engraving of the "Elevation du cimetière de la ville de Chaux," [Plate 100] where the earth, like the cemetery, is half-buried in the clouds, surrounded by the planets each marked by its appropriate astrological sign. This image summarises Ledoux's aspirations for an *architecture parlante*: sublime in its vastness and simplicity, yet presenting an immediately recognisable symbolic form. Its stark poetry rejects all direct reference to history, either of the antiquarian kind as practised by Court de Gebelin or Viel de Saint-Maux, or of the overtly "Egyptianising" motifs of Boullée. For Ledoux it stands as a mediating figure, balanced between heaven and earth, the sign of a nature that, were it not for the architect, would be no more than a vast cemetery.

Below:
Cemetery
of the city
of Chaux,
elevation.
From: *L'Architecture...*,
Plate 100.

Right page:
Cemetery
of the city
of Chaux,
plan and section.
From: *L'Architecture...*,
Plate 99.

Following double page:
Church
of the city
of Chaux,
perspective view.
From: *L'Architecture...*,
Plate 72.

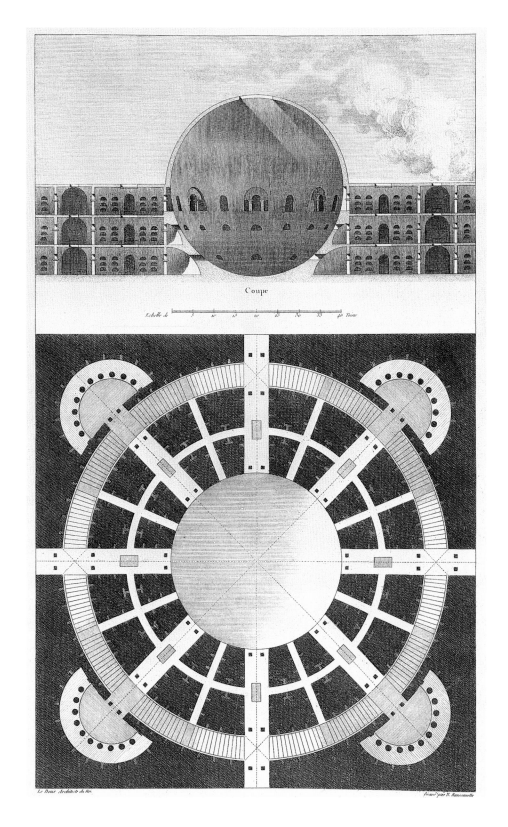

Coupe

Echelle de   Toises

Le Doux Architecte du Roi.   Gravé par N. Ransonnette.

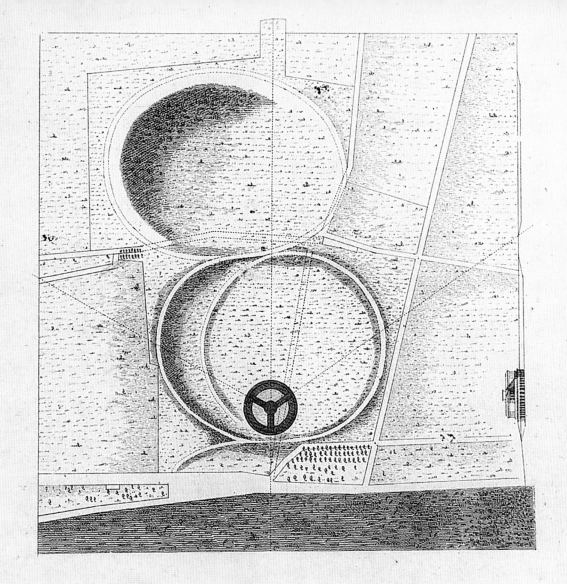

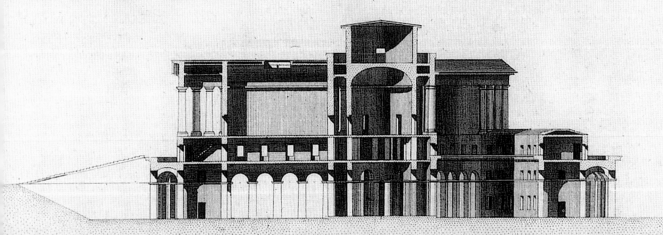

13. UTOPIA OR REVOLUTION

"Fateful events cut short the thread of my work before the autumn of my life. Suddenly positions obtained by hard work passed into sacrilegious hands; I lost the fruits of thirty years of honourable service." [33]

Throughout the Revolutionary years and the foundation of the Empire, Ledoux was left virtually without work, friends or money. His close affiliation with the courts of Louis XV and Louis XVI and especially with the hated figure of Madame du Barry, his rumoured connections with the aristocracy in exile (notably with Calonne in London) and, most of all, his reputation as architect of the Ferme rendered him unemployable and forced him into a kind of internal exile. Nevertheless, in the first months after July 1789, and despite his dismissal from the *barrières*, he clung to a guarded optimism, pressing his claim for reimbursement and continuing to correspond with the contractors in Aix. From the *entresol* of the Palais Royal, in the company of Joseph Vernet the painter and Le Peletier de Saint-Fargeau, soon to become a martyr of the Revolution, Ledoux observed the daily events that, while touching him, had not yet entirely destroyed him. As always he chose the way of cautious reform: the Club de Valois, of which he was a member, under the patronage of the Duc d'Orléans, numbered Condorcet, La Rochefoucauld, Sieyès and the Duc de Montmorency among its members. By

Left page:
Museum, site plan, section.
From: Gallet (ed.),
Architecture de Ledoux.
Inédits pour un Tome III,
Plate 27, Paris,
Les Editions du
Demi-Cercle, 1991.

Above:
Perspective view
of a country house.
From: Gallet (ed.),
Architecture de Ledoux.
Inédits pour un Tome III,
Plate 73, Paris,
Les Editions du
Demi-Cercle, 1991.

the beginning of 1792, indeed, Ledoux had even modestly re-established his practice, with the commission for fifteen houses for the rich sugar-planter, Jean-Baptiste Hosten. This development, including Hosten's own house, was planned, like many of the London terraces wherein so many of Ledoux's former patrons had found shelter, around a landscape garden with miniature temples and *fabriques* disguising carriage-houses and a "serpentine" pool with a bridge over the centre. Four of the houses, raised on a high rusticated ground floor, formed a linked series, separated by indented courtyard. The style was Palladian, with motifs and decoration abstracted; inside, the decor was lifted from Herculaneum, Ledoux's last gesture to a newly discovered history, with paintings by Hubert Robert.

By mid-year, Ledoux felt confident enough to buy a new property and press his candidacy for first-class membership of the Academy of Architecture, only to be thwarted at the last minute by David's successful campaign for closing the Academies. But this moment of respite rapidly disappeared: in August his wife died, already separated from him and living in the house of Jean Monclar, the former contractor for the Saline. In the beginning of 1793, Ledoux was already taking out loans from various friends. On 29 November, he was finally arrested together with fourteen other suspected inhabitants of the quarter by the Comité Révolutionnaire of the Faubourg du Nord and seemed about to suffer the fate of so many of his former friends and patrons. Despite his later dissimulation ("I was interrupted …" he writes simulating a break in the narrative of *L'Architecture*, "The national axe was raised, they called for Ledoux, but it was not me; my conscience, my star of fortune guided me: it was a doctor of the Sorbonne with the same names. Unhappy victim! … I continue:" [401]) his captors were in fact well aware of his past. They accused him of working for the ex-nobles, notably for Madame du Barry; of continuing a style of life not in keeping with an out-of-work architect, of retaining a cook, coachman and servant; of still pressing his claim for the *barrières*; of applying for the *cordon noir* in 1788, and of being a member of the Club de Valois. Nor had he sufficiently demonstrated a change of attitude after 1789, or voiced his wholehearted support for the execution of Louis XVI.[1] Ledoux, helped for the moment by his daughter Alexandrine, prepared his defence; a letter from her in July 1794 responded to the accusations, and was followed by many touching pleas from the two motherless daughters who could not live without so dear a father – emotions soon forgotten in the later struggles over their inheritance.[2]

Ledoux took an entirely practical approach: in his view, as he noted in the many letters he composed asking for his release, he had already demonstrated the value of his work, searching for the true principles of architecture for more than twenty years; he had presented the committee with the drafts of his great book; requesting permission to continue his essentially "Republican" work, he asked for the notes and drawings still in his house under seal; finally, in a letter written eight days before the condemnation of Robespierre, the 1st Thermidor, he offered his designs for agricultural institutions, public baths and the like in exchange for his freedom.

Released, not for any of these promises but after the fall of Robespierre, on 13th January 1795, Ledoux was immediately faced with a ten-year legal battle fought by his younger daughter to retrieve her mother's legacy, rightly fearful that it was likely to be consumed by the costs of engraving Ledoux's ideal projects. For during his year in prison, Ledoux had advanced the state of his text, outlining a never-to-be-published memoranda on the *barrières*, and planning a five-volume publication of his work. He was to spend the final eleven years of his life completing this task, amassing the plates, publishing a *Prospectus* in 1802, and the first volume in 1804. Ledoux, despite financial insecurity was triumphant. This was a work that would justify him to posterity. He wrote to Mignard, the contractor for Aix in 1803: "it is written with energy and a good tone. It has been printed and is of the highest quality: I think it will have a great effect."[3] In the *Prospectus*, Ledoux compared himself to the awakening Epi-

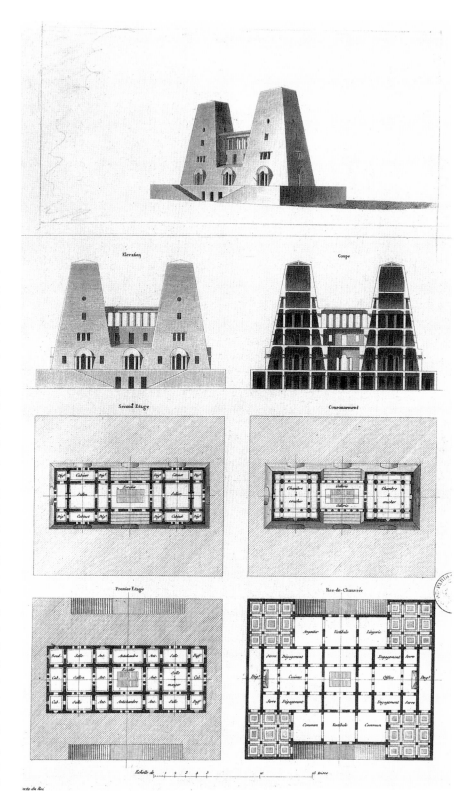

Perspective view
of a country house,
before 1792.
From: Gallet (ed.),
*Architecture de Ledoux.
Inédits pour un Tome III*,
Plate 71, Paris,
Les Editions du
Demi-Cercle, 1991.

menides of Knossos, founder of Orphism: an analogy that returned him to the entry gate of his first great commission, the Saline de Chaux. The reviews of the first volume were indeed generally favourable, even if that published in the *Journal des bâtiments* seems to have been largely written by Ledoux himself.

Ledoux's book had undergone many changes since he had first conceived it as a collection of his built and projected works in the early 1780s: many times announced, this collection of plates had, in different combinations been presented, without text to successive ministers of finance, and selected patrons – Paul of Russia, who had accepted the dedication in 1782, finally received 273 drawings in the Spring of 1789. The first engraved title page dates from that year; simply called *L'Architecture de C.N. Ledoux*, it listed what it termed a "collection that brings together all the kinds of building used in the social order," built or begun between 1768 and 1789. It seems that the qualification "First Volume" was only added at a later date. The list of contents makes no mention of the ideal city, but is restricted to real commissions. Gradually, during the Revolution, the text took on a more elaborate theoretical and literary shape. Ledoux brought together fragments of his writing – letters to clients and friends, justificatory *mémoires*, official reports, some from as early as 1776 – inserting them in a continuous meditation on architecture and his

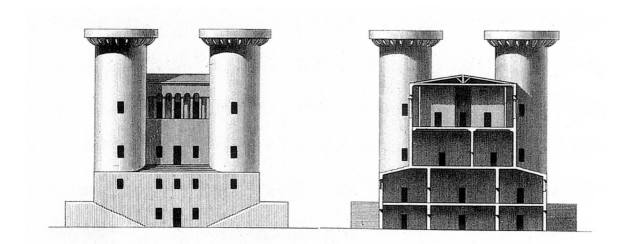

career. The first indication of this change appeared in a summary applying for his membership in the newly created Institut de France, in September 1800, that corroborated Ledoux's statements from prison: the work was now to be called *Architecture sentimentale, contenant tous les genres d'édifices connus dans l'ordre social* and announced in six volumes.[4]

Clearly Ledoux was now referring to a theoretical treatise that dealt with the effect of art and architecture on the sensations, the psychological aesthetics of Condillac and Helvétius, given literary expression by Delille, Rousseau, Watelet, and Le Camus de Mézières and, in the unpublished essay well known to his circle before his death in 1799, Boullée. Ledoux was now in full competition with his fellow academicians: he termed the work, which now expanded the list of building-types and projects previously announced, "an Encyclopaedia or Architectural Museum." Conceived now as the architectural equivalent to Diderot's *Encyclopédie*, Ledoux's placed his book in the general context of the emergence of the "museum" as a didactic institution. Blondel had dreamed of establishing a museum of models for student instruction; Louis-François Cassas was in the process of building his own collection, later to be exhibited in 1806; the Louvre was gradually taking on all the characteristics of a historical museum for art, exhibiting the spoils of

Napoleon's expeditions to Egypt and Italy, and Alexandre Lenoir had already opened his popular Musée des Monuments Français to the public. In the draft of the *Prospectus*, Ledoux stated clearly his views on the relations of architecture to society; the work would treat of "social virtues," "political economy," "commerce and industry" – indeed all the "progressive ideas" joined to the major philosophic currents of the Enlightenment. These would, he stated, following the method of the *philosophes*, be returned to their "origins": "To the origins of everything, of the first religions adapted to morality, of architecture, its progress and deviations … The moral and philosophical aim of the work, all supported on the principles of nature, returned to the universal system that constitutes the happiness of the greatest number."

From the origins of architecture in the first religions to its subsequent progress; from its natural principles to its role of ensuring the happiness of the greatest number; architecture was thereby brought into the centre of philosophical and moral concern somewhere between Diderot and Bentham. The final title of the work, *L'Architecture considérée sous le rapport de l'art, des moeurs et de la législation*, playing on similar titles invented by Bentham, Madame de Staël and the prize competitions for the Institut, confirmed Ledoux's grand aims. It was this peculiar mixture of Enlight-

enment rigorism and pre-Romantic sentimentality that made Ledoux's text, already allusive enough in its language, conceptually difficult for his contemporaries who founded the myth of an "unreadable Ledoux." Nevertheless, many of his literary contemporaries appreciated his poetics of architecture as a true utopia, in the grand tradition from antiquity through the Renaissance. The Abbé Delille, in his long prose poem *L'Imagination* inserted a long homage to his architect friend; in a note to the later publication of this poem, Delille's editor, M. de Choiseul-Gouffier, wrote: "[Ledoux] did not cease to perfect the plans for an imaginary city … this was a veritable utopia of architecture; and this work should be dedicated to the Republic of Plato."[5]

Others saw more recent references. A biographical fragment, discovered by the historian Paul Turner in the papers of François-Joseph Bélanger, describes Ledoux as profoundly influenced by the celebrated Renaissance treatise, *Hypnerotomachia Poliphili*, generally attributed to one Francesco Colonna and published in 1499. Some time after the death of Ledoux, Bélanger noted that his friend "was inspired by the *Rêves de Polifi* [sic] for the text of *L'Architecture*, thinking that it was a suitable frame for his work." Immediately, Bélanger recollected, Ledoux "relinquished his pencils in favour of his pen."[6] Bélanger attributed what he called the "new language" of Ledoux

Left page and right:
Elevation, section
and plan of a
country house.
From: Gallet (ed.),

Architecture de Ledoux.
Inédits pour un Tome III,
Plate 73, Paris,
Les Editions du
Demi-Cercle, 1991.

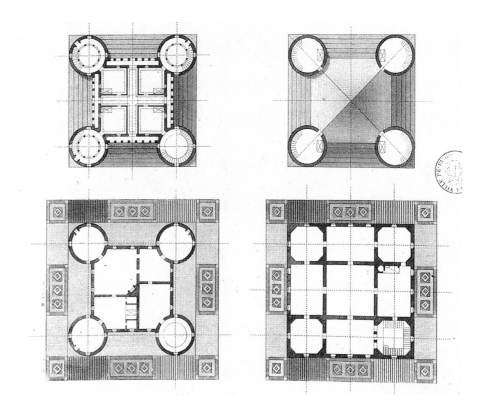

and his strange style, illustrating his "over-exalted imagination," to his fascination for the work to which he doubtless referred: *Hypnerotomachia Poliphili* or "Songe de Poliphile."[7]

Bélanger's note confirms that the Renaissance, and especially the French Renaissance, had an influence on Ledoux that has generally been ignored because of his evident nostalgia for the classicism of the seventeenth century and his evident affinities with the Enlightenment. In fact, however, there was a growing interest in Colonna's text towards the end of the Ancien Régime, an interest that culminated in a new translation by the architect-historian and supporter of Ledoux, Jacques-Guillaume Legrand.[8] Published in 1804, the same year as *L'Architecture*, it had been read aloud by Legrand to the circle of readers of the Philotechnical Society that gathered in the former Maison Thélusson, a society that had succeeded the Athenaeum, of which Ledoux had been a member.[9] Indeed the two texts, the *Hypnerotomachia* and *L'Architecture*, have many points in common, beyond the similarity of tone and theme, and it is clear that Ledoux was drawn to paraphrase entire passages, even to the extent of setting his ideal town in a dream-like setting like the one described by Colonna.[10]

But beyond the atmosphere of dream that suffused the two works – dreams suspended between a rediscovered antiquity and everyday life in the present, and a utopian future – other precise resemblances can be discerned. The most evident are the scenes, often repeated in both texts, that describe the awakening of the narrator. Legrand's translation begins: "The dawn seemed to promise a delightful day: a soft languor took over all my senses." [LH 1] Ledoux's text is full of similar moments, as when, the "traveller" visiting the utopia of Chaux "awakes at the first light of dawn: the air is pure, the earth, dampened by the abundant dew, seems to be covered with the jewels of the morning." [170]

Even the sites of Poliphilo's dream and those of Ledoux's traveller are similar. Poliphilo thinks that he is "transported into a vast plain covered with flowers, and embroidered with greenery," [LH 3] while Ledoux, visiting the construction site of the salt works writes: "Already the Zephyrs emerge from their retreats, and the freshness of the morning extends across the plain." [78]

In both cases, these openings announce the beginning of a dream narrative, conceived as a kind of voyage of initiation. Beyond this, one might compare the oval plan of the labyrinth in the *Hypnerotomachia*, in the form of "the elliptical heavens," with its "small canal bordered by an agreeable meadow … decorated with fountains, statues, and other riches of art" [LH 88] that stand in the midst of its pathways, with the town that Ledoux depicts on the *Carte des environs de la ville de Chaux* [Pl. 14]. Ledoux's town is similarly described as an ellipse that follows the trajectory of the sun traced on the earth [LH 100-101]. Joining his plan for a new town to a more general cosmological symbolism, Ledoux draws the comparison between its form and that of a dewdrop shining in the first rays of the dawn, and that of the sun itself. [69] There is also a striking resemblance between the pyramidal monument placed on a cubic base encountered

Left:
Mezzanine, ground floor,
first floor and basement
plans of a country house.
From: Gallet (ed.),
Architecture de Ledoux.
Inédits pour un Tome III,
Plate 77, Paris,
Les Editions du
Demi-Cercle, 1991.

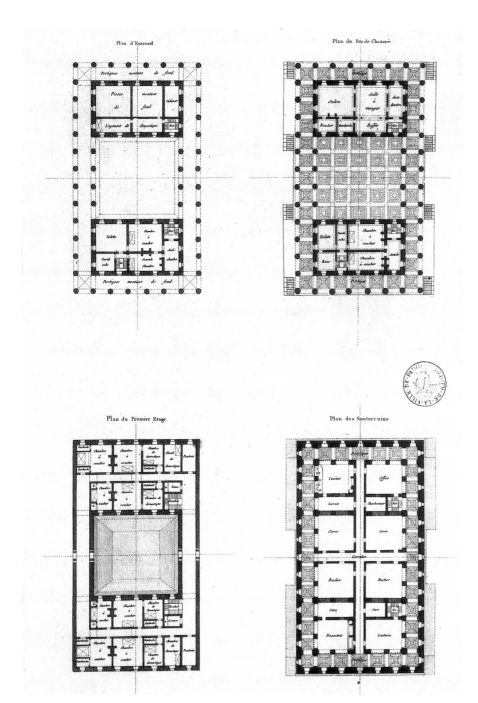

by Polyphilo and the multiple variations on this theme in Ledoux as a "symbolic system," a code of signification equally espoused by Colonna, who wrote: "In these three primary figures, the square, the circle, and the triangle ... there consists the entire celestial harmony." [LH 99-100] To this responds the conviction of Ledoux according to which "the circle, the square... are the letters of the alphabet that authors use in the texture of their best works," [135] an alphabet that he uses in the most symbolic of the institutions of Chaux, notably the Panarèthéon. "The form of the cube is the symbol of immutability," wrote Ledoux, "one seats the gods and heroes on a cube." [185] Ledoux refers throughout his text to such "primary ideas,"[52] seeming to follow the lessons of Colonna, who also associates geometrical volumes to "first ideas": "These primary truths ... draw me to associate sublime ideas to simple forms made up of a few stones cut geometrically." [LH 101]

Nevertheless, perhaps the most striking resemblance is the common theme of a "voyage of love." "Love" is the explicit subject of the *Hyp-nerotomachia*, but as many historians have noted, the allegory covers the real passion nourished by Colonna for the architecture of antiquity and its ruins. Ledoux seems to press this analogy further in order to express the total identification of the architect with his creation. Indeed, Ledoux took for himself Colonna's principal maxim. In the

Perspective view
of a country house,
after 1792,
engraved by Geoffroy.
From: Gallet (ed.),

Architecture de Ledoux.
Inédits pour un Tome III,
Plate 77, Paris,
Les Editions du
Demi-Cercle, 1991.

latter's fable, Poliphilo and Polia are transported through a storm in Cupid's boat; at the height of the tempest a banner unfurls with the inscription, drawn from Horace: *Omnia vincit amor*. This refers not only to the theme of Chapter 20, Book 1 of the *Hypnerotomachia* describing the triumph of the "pilot of love" over the tempests of life, but also to a motif that recurs throughout the book. [LH Vol. II, 50] It is certainly not by chance that Ledoux selected the same motto for his own book as an epigraph to his introduction, *Omnia vincit amor*, adding in a note: "It is this sentiment which has inspired and sustained me in this long work."[1] Equally, we cannot underestimate the importance of the site of the salt works itself, which by a happy coincidence was popularly called the "Vallon de l'Amour." [73]

It was, finally, in the project for the Oikéma, that "fragment of a Greek monument," that Ledoux imagined Hymen and Love drawing up a peace treaty intended to "purify public morality and render mankind happier." [199] In Ledoux's terms, the architect "like the sun when it bathes in the ocean waves in order to purify its brilliant rays," is "more powerful than Love" itself, as he designs a temple that bears on its pediment the inscription "Here are implanted the mobile graces in order to eternalise virtue" [203] and whose phallic plan celebrates the reign of Priapus in the Garden of Love, also a central leitmotif of Colonna's Temple of Priapus in the gardens of the *Hyp-*

nerotomachia. One imagines that Ledoux would have been inspired by the echo of the melodious voice of Polia from Cupid's boat as she sang of "the riches that ornament the cities, the beauty of the countrysides, the majesty of the arts, the rich tableaux of nature, and everything that Jupiter created in order to ennoble the pleasures of mankind."[LH 51]

In the light of Ledoux's passion for the *Hypnerotomachia*, the ideal city of Chaux reveals a more classically utopian aspect than scholars have hitherto imagined. Certainly it celebrates the ideals of the century of the Enlightenment, echoing the progressive convictions of the circle of Trudaine and Turgot; and Ledoux no doubt felt sincere when he affirmed his "Republicanism" to the Revolutionary authorities. But in his desire to emulate the narrative form and quasi-mystical content of the *Hypnerotomachia*, Ledoux revealed his allegiance to the very principles of classicism and utopianism that the Enlightenment had sought to eradicate. The nostalgia for the seventeenth century evinced by his architectural motifs and textual references is here expressed in the dream of an eternal and omnipresent Arcadia, as if the *fabriques* of Chaux were sited in a landscape painted by Poussin. It is thus not perhaps by chance that this architect, of whom it was said in prison that he spoke and dreamed only of "columns," and whose protectors were named Colonia and Calonne, found his ultimate inspi-

ration in the work of a dreamer called Colonna.[11]

For more than two years after the publication of *L'Architecture* Ledoux lived in hopes, waiting for a recognition that never came; his idealism and social utopianism found few admirers in the milieu of *le style Empire*. A long review by the architect Détournelle summarised the work, and found it both difficult and useful. An anonymous reviewer in 1804 was more appreciative of what he called Ledoux's "architectural metaphysics," and figurative style.[12]

Optimistic to the last, Ledoux received the new mayor of Aix in 1803; he continued to see old friends – Delille had returned from exile in 1802, and Le Roy and Vaudoyer tried to interest him in a new venture, their Société Académique d'Architecture in 1806. He took part in a jury at the École Impériale des Beaux-Arts, and even, in the last year of his life, renewed his professional qualifications by taking out a patent. On the 12th November 1806, having been ill for some months, he made his will dividing his goods between his surviving daughter and his protégé Pierre Vignon; seven days later he died of a paralysis. His funeral, despite the rain, attracted a large crowd who followed the cortege on foot to Montmartre; eulogies and poems were read by Luce de Lancival and Vignon, and a student competition was announced in Ledoux's name, with a copy of *L'Architecture* as a second prize; it is improbable that the reward was ever claimed.

NOTES

PREFACE TO THE ENGLISH EDITION / INTRODUCTION

1 The most complete monographs on Ledoux are: *Michel Gallet, Claude-Nicolas Ledoux 1736-1806* (Paris, 1980); Anthony Vidler, *Claude-Nicolas Ledoux. Architecture and Social Reform at the End of the Ancien Régime* (Cambridge, Mass., 1990); Daniel Rabreau, *Claude-Nicolas Ledoux (1736-1806). L'Architecture et les fastes du temps* (Paris, 2000). The following essay is a concise version of my research that was published more extensively in my monograph of 1990. It was originally published in French in 1987 and now revised and brought up to date with respect to recent literature. All three works contain full bibliographies.

2 Victor Hugo, "Guerre au démolisseurs!" (1825-32), from *Littérature et philosophie mêlées*, in *Oeuvres complètes: Critique*, presentation by Jean-Pierre Reynaud (Paris, 1985), p. 187.

3 Antoine-Chrysostôme Quatremère de Quincy, article "Barrière," *Encyclopédie méthodique; Architecture*, 3 vols. (Paris, 1788-1825), vol. 1, p. 216.

4 [Léon Vaudoyer], *Magasin pittoresque* 20 (1852), p. 187.

5 Emil Kaufmann, *Von Ledoux bis Le Corbusier: Ursprung und Entwicklung der autonomen Architektur* (Vienna and Leipzig, 1933).

6 See Hans Sedlmayr, Verlust der Mitte (Salzburg, Vienna, 1948), English edition: *Art in Crisis: The Lost Centre* (London, 1956).

7 Michel Gallet, *Claude-Nicolas Ledoux, 1736-1806* (Paris, 1980).

8 See Monique Mosser, et al., *Piranèse et les Français* (Rome, Dijon, Paris, 1976).

9 Michel Gallet, "Palladio et l'architecture française dans la seconde moitié du XVIIIe siècle," *Monuments historiques*, 2 (1975), pp. 43-55.

10 Colen Campbell, John Woolfe, James Gandon, *Vitruvius Britannicus* (London, 1769); Jacques-François Blondel, *L'Architecture française*, 4 vols. (Paris, 1752-1756).

11 See Roland Barthes, "Les planches de l'Encyclopédie," *Le degré zéro de l'écriture suivi de Nouveaux essais critiques* (Paris, 1972), pp. 89-105, English edition: *Writing degree zero, and Elements of semiology* (Boston, 1970).

1. CLASSICAL MAXIMS

1 Claude-Nicolas Ledoux, *L'Architecture considérée sous le rapport de l'art, des moeurs et de la législation* (Paris, 1804). The numbers placed in parentheses following the citations or plates of Ledoux correspond to the pagination of the only volume published in Ledoux's lifetime. The latest reprint edition is published by Hermann (Paris, 1997). Where indicated, the references to plate numbers are to the edition by Daniel Ramée, *Architecture de C.N. Ledoux*, 2 vols. (Paris, 1847) or Michel Gallet, ed., *Architecture de*

Ledoux. Inédits pour un tome III (Paris, 1991). The Ramée edition was reprinted, with an introduction by the author, by Princeton Architectural Press (New York, 1983).

2 For an account of the early career of Ledoux see "J.C" [Jacques Cellerier], *Notice rapide sur la vie et les ouvrages de Claude-Nicolas Ledoux* (Paris, 1806).

3 See Jean-Baptiste Crévier, *Histoire de l'Université de Paris, depuis son origine jusqu'en l'année 1600*, 7 vols. (Paris, 1761), vol. 2, pp. 464 ff.

4 This revision of the programme in order to introduce the "Moderns" was accomplished by Charles Rollin, whose pedagogical methods, derived from the "Little Schools" of Port Royal, were lauded by Ledoux in his text.

5 See George Snyders, *La pédagogie en France au XVIIe et XVIIIe siècles* (Paris, 1965); César Chesneau Dumarsais published his popular *Traité des tropes* in 1730.

6 Jacques-François Blondel opened his course of public lectures on architecture in 1743; by the mid-1750s his school had gained a reputation as an enlightened alternative to the school of the Académie d'Architecture. Blondel contributed to the first seven volumes of the *Encyclopédie* and taught most of the prominent architects of the period including Boullée, Patte, Trouard, de Wailly, Antoine, de Neufforge, Peyre, Desprez, Brongniart, Rondelet, Legrand, Molinos, Huvé, Potain and Gondouin, many of whom would become friends and colleagues of Ledoux.

7 Barthes, "Les planches," op. cit.

8 Jacques-François Blondel, *Cours d'architecture, ou traité de la décoration, distribution et construction des bâtiments; contenant les leçons données en 1750*, 9 vols. (Paris, 1771-1777). See also Robin Middleton, "Jacques-François Blondel and the *Cours d'architecture*," *Journal of the Society of Architectural Historians* 17 (December 1959).

9 For an exhaustive discussion of these terms, see Werner Szambien, *Symétrie, goût, caractère* (Paris, 1986).

10 Blondel, *Cours d'architecture*, 2 vols. (Paris 1771), p. 229.

11 See Anthony Vidler, "The Idea of Type: Transformations in the Academic Ideal," *Oppositions* 8 (1977).

12 Michel Foucault, *Les mots et les choses* (Paris, 1966), p. 158, English edition: *The Order of Things: An Archaeology of the Human Sciences* (London, 1970).

13 Jean le Rond d'Alembert, *Discours préliminaire de l'Encyclopédie* [1751] (Paris: Gonthier, 1965), p. 49.

14 See Jean-Jacques Rousseau, *Discours sur les sciences et les arts* [1750]; Denis Diderot, *Salon de Paris 1765* [1765] (Paris: Hermann, 1984) and article "Vérité," *Encyclopédie* vol. XVII, p. 364.

15 Pierre Patte, *Monuments érigés en France à la gloire de Louis XV* (Paris, 1765).

16 Marc-Antoine Laugier, *Essai sur L'Architecture* (Paris, 1753, 1755), English edition: *Essay on Architecture* (Los Angeles, 1977).

2. EMBLEMS OF NOBILITY

1   François Furet and Denis Richet, *La Révolution Française* [1965-66] (Paris, 1973), p. 28, English edition: *The French Revolution* (London, 1970).
2   Élie Fréron, *Année littéraire*, VI (1762), p. 282.
3   One might compare the café of Ledoux with that of Piranesi, constructed three years earlier in Rome, the Caffé degli Inglesi, where the decoration was entirely historicist, surrounding the room with a panorama of "Egyptian" architectural scenes.
4   Michel Gallet, "La jeunesse de Ledoux," *Gazette des beaux-arts* (February, 1970), pp. 1-92; "Ledoux et sa clientèle parisienne," *Bulletin de la Société de l'histoire de Paris 1974-75* (1976), pp. 131-73.
5   See C. Rivière, *Un village de Brie au XVIIIe siècle: Maupertuis* (Paris, 1939).
6   Summarised in a letter of Ledoux to the Académie d'Architecture of November 1767; Archives de l'Institut, B21, published in Gallet, *Claude-Nicolas Ledoux*, p. 263. Daniel Ramée published the "House of the Agricultural Guards of Maupertuis," in his republication of *L'Architecture* with additional plates, *Architecture de C.N. Ledoux* 2 vols. (Paris, 1847), vol. 2, plate 254.
7   The circle of Montesquiou is described by Madame Vigée-Lebrun in her *Souvenirs*, vol. 1, p. 106, cited in Jacques Silvestre de Sacy, *Alexandre-Théodore Brongniart (1739-1813)* (Paris, 1940), p. 55.
8   Edmond de Goncourt, *La Guimard* (Paris, 1893).
9   Edmond de Goncourt, *La du Barry* (Paris, 1878).
10 Jean-François de Bastide, *La petite maison* (Paris, 1753; 1879). For Fragonard's work at Louveciennes see Franklin M. Biebel, "Fragonard et Madame du Barry," *Gazette des beaux-arts* 1101 (1960), pp. 207-225.
11 J.B.L. Coquereau, *Mémoires de l'Abbé Terray*, vol. 1 (Paris, 1776), p. 271.

3. PUBLIC ADMINISTRATION

1   Gallet, "La jeunesse de Ledoux," op.cit.
2   See Bruno Fortier, "La nascità dell'Ecole des Ponts et Chaussées," parts 1 and 2, *Casabella* 495-496 (October-November, 1983), pp. 40-47; 36-45.
3   Johannes Langner, "La vue par-dessous le pont," *Actes du colloques Piranèse et les Français* (Rome, 1978).
4   Arrêt du conseil, Versailles, September 20, 1771, signed by de Maupeou and the Abbé Terray. Archives Nationales, E2474.
5   Trudaine de Montigny, son of Daniel Trudaine (friend of Perronet and supporter of the Ponts et Chaussées), was a friend of Diderot, translator of Lessing, and a member of Turgot's circle. Haudry de Soucy, Farmer General, was in turn a friend of Trudaine, and of the Thélusson family, to whom he recommended Ledoux in 1778.

4. THE ARCHITECTURE OF PRODUCTION

1   See the article "Salines," *Encyclopédie*, XIV (1765), pp. 544-569, by Dupin and de Falbaire de Quingey; Pierre Boyé, *Les salines et le sel en Lorraine au XVIIIe siècle* (Nancy, 1901); Guy Nicot, "Les salines d'Arc-et-Senans," *Monuments historiques*, no. 2 (1978), pp. 33-48.
2   Arrêt du Conseil, 29 April 1773, Archives Départementales du Jura, C 406, folio 4. See Abbé Lédontal, *Arc-et-Senans à travers les âges* (Besançon, 1927).
3   For a detailed account of these wooden constructions, see Pierre Lacroix, *La saline d'Arc-et-Senans et les techniques de canalisation en bois: notes d'histoire comtoise* (Lons-le-Saunier, 1970).
4   Blondel, *Cours d'architecture* vol. II, pp. 398-399.
5   *Traité pour la construction d'une saline en Franche-Comté, son exploitation et celle des autres salines de la même province* (Paris, 1774), Archives Nationales, G1 93.
6   Ledoux was asked, with Chalgrin, to prepare a report on the re-building of the Hôtel-Dieu after the fire of 1772; see E. Chambardel, "Une solution inédite des problèmes de gestion hospitalière," *L'Hôpital et l'aide sociale*, 23 (1963).
7   Michel Foucault, Bruno Fortier et al., *Les machines à guérir. Aux origines de l'hôpital moderne* (Brussels, 1979).
8   Antoine Petit, *Mémoire sur la meilleure manière de construire un hôpital de malades* (Paris, 1774), p. 5.
9   Claude Perrault, trad., Vitruvius, *Les dix livres d'architecture* (Paris, 1673), plates XLII, XLIV, XLV, English edition: *The Ten Books of Architecture* (New York, 1986).
10 See Monika Steinhauser and Daniel Rabreau, "Le théâtre de l'Odéon de Charles de Wailly et Marie-Joseph Peyre, 1767-1782," *Revue de l'art* 19 (1973), pp. 9-49.
11 Julien-David Le Roy, *Les ruines des plus beaux monuments de la Grèce* (Paris, 1758 and 1774).
12 A motif often used to designate salt works in the late Renaissance: the upturned urn was equally used at Salins.
13 Michel Foucault, *Surveiller et punir. Naissance de la prison* (Paris, 1975), p. 176, English edition: *Discipline and Punish: The Birth of the Prison* (New York, 1977).
14 See Anthony Vidler, "The Architecture of the Lodges," *Oppositions* 5 (New York, 1976).
15 Servandoni had already presented "The descent of Orpheus into the Underworld" as a spectacle in the Tuileries in 1740; the reviewer of Gluck's opera in 1774 remembered this scene with admiration.
16 Jean-Jacques Rousseau, *Discours sur l'origine et les fondements de l'inégalité parmi les hommes* [1755] (Paris, 1980), p. 208.
17 Article "Manufacture," *Encyclopédie*, X, p. 60.
18 Archives Départementales du Jura, 8J 323.
19 *Ouvriers de la saline de Montmorot*, 26 February-26 June 1776, Archives Départementales du Jura, 8J 440.
20 See L. Mazoyer, "Exploitation forestière et conflits sociaux en Franche-Comté," *Annales E.S.C.* IV (1932), pp. 339ff; S. Monniot, "Le rôle de la fôret dans la vie des populations Franc-comtoises de la conquête française à la Révolution 1674-1789," *Revue d'histoire moderne* (September-December 1937), pp. 449ff.

5. LANGUAGES OF CHARACTER

1   See J.M. Dudot, B. Flouzat, et al., *Le devoir d'embellir*, CORDA (Nancy, 1977).
2   See Pierre Patte, *Mémoires sur les objets les plus importants de L'Architecture* (Paris, 1769) and Abbé Charles-François de Lubersac, *Discours sur les monuments publics de tous les âges* (Paris, 1775).
3   Anthony Vidler, *The Writing of the Walls: Architectural Theory in the Late Enlightenment* (New York, 1989).
4   Edmund Burke, *A Philosophical Enquiry into the Origin of Our Ideas of the Sublime and Beautiful*, ed. J. Boulton [1757] (London, 1958), pp. 74-82.

6. GALLO-ROMAN ANTIQUITY

1   Such enthusiasm for the Roman antiquities on French soil was shared by an increasing number of scholars of the time: see Charles-Louis Clérisseau, *Les monuments de Nîmes* with a *Texte historique et descriptif* by Jacques-Guillaume Legrand (Paris, 1778-1804).
2   Jean-Baptiste de La Curne de Sainte-Palaye, *Mémoires sur l'ancienne chevalerie considérée comme un établissement politique et militaire*, 2 vols. (Paris, 1759).

7. THEATRICAL VISION

1   See J. Rittaud-Hutinet, *La vision du futur: Ledoux et ses théâtres* (Lyon, 1982).
2   Charles-André de Lacoré, 24 August 1775, Archives du Doubs, C40. Republished in Rittaud-Hutinet, pp. 132-33 and Gallet, *Ledoux*, p. 267.
3   See Henri Lagrave, *Le théâtre et le public à Paris de 1715-1750* (Paris, 1972).
4   See Yvon Belaval, *L'esthétique sans paradoxe de Diderot* (Paris, 1983) and Denis Diderot, "Entretiens sur *Le fils naturel*" [1757] and "De la poésie dramatique" [1758], in *Oeuvres esthétiques*, ed. Paul Vernière (Paris, 1959).
5   Jean-Claude Bonnet, "Introduction" to Denis Diderot, *Le neveu de Rameau* (Paris, 1983), p. 35.
6   See Daniel Rabreau, "Autour du voyage d'Italie" (1750): Soufflot, Cochin et M. de Marigny réformateurs de l'architecture théâtrale française," *Bollettino del centro internazionale di studi di architettura Andrea Palladio* 17 (1975), pp. 213-25.
7   Charles-Nicolas Cochin, Jérôme-Charles Bellicard, *Observations sur les antiquités de la ville d'Herculanum* (Paris, 1754), p. 10.

8 Pierre Patte, *Essai sur L'Architecture théâtrale* (Paris, 1782), p.126.

9 Ledoux to de Lacoré, 24 August 1775, Archives du Doubs, C40.

10 Ibid.

11 Jean-Jacques Rousseau, *Lettre à M. d'Alembert sur son article "Genève"* (Lettre sur les *spectacles*), (Paris, 1758), and idem., *Julie ou la Nouvelle Héloïse* (Paris, 1761).

12 Helen Leclerc, "Au théâtre de Besançon (1775-1784): Claude-Nicolas Ledoux, réformateur et précurseur de Richard Wagner," *Revue d'histoire du théâtre* 10 (1958), pp. 103-27.

13 Charles-Nicolas Cochin, *Projet d'une salle de spectacle pour un théâtre de comédie* (Paris, 1765).

14 Guillaume Dard de Bosco, "Observations sur le service du théâtre," February 1785, Archives Municipales de Besançon, DD 35, 123.

15 Ernest de Ganay, "La salle de spectacle de l'architecte Ledoux à Besançon," *Revue de l'art ancien et moderne* 52 (June-December, 1927), pp. 2-21; on p. 17 Ganay cites the account of the lawyer Grimont, whose manuscript journal is conserved in the Bibliothèque de Besançon.

16 Ibid.

17 Daniel Rabreau, "Des scènes figurées à la mise en scène du monument urbain," in *Actes du colloque "Piranèse et les Français"* (Rome, 1978) and in *Claude-Nicolas Ledoux (1736-1806): L'Architecture et les fastes du temps* (Paris, 2000), pp. 142-147.

18 See Kurt W. Forster, "Schinkel's Panoramic Planning of Central Berlin," *Modulus* 16 (1983), p. 65.

19 Such aerial aspirations were, as Rabreau has pointed out, always brought down to earth by Ledoux – as in the "Coupe du théâtre de Besançon prise sur la largeur," showing the basilical mise en scène, which at the same time places the audience, figuratively seated at the end of the basilica on stage, into the theater of the city itself, as it depicts the new square in which the theatre is to be sited: Rabreau, *Ledoux*, p. 143.

8. PHYSIOGNOMIES OF JUSTICE

1 The fundamental study of Ledoux's work in Aix is Jean-Jacques Gloton and Serge Conard, "Aix-en-Provence dans l'oeuvre de Claude-Nicolas Ledoux," in *Monuments et mémoires publiés par l'Académie des inscriptions et belles-lettres* (Vendôme, 1983), pp. 55-150; more recently Marie Bels, *Sur les traces de Ledoux* (Marseille, 2004) has studied the development of the designs for the Palais de Justice and Prisons in the context of 18th century typological theory and published all the relevant drawings from Ledoux's atelier in magnificent color.

2 See J.-P. Coste, *Aix en 1765: Structure urbaine et société* (Aix-en-Provence, 1970), especially pp. 195ff. and 230ff. For the functions of the parliament, see Sharon Kettering, *Judicial Politics and Urban Revolt in Seventeenth-Century France: The Parliament of Aix, 1629-1659* (Princeton, 1978).

3 Ledoux, "Report," October-November 1784, Archives Nationales, H1 1359, published in full in Gloton and Conard, "Aix-en-Provence," p. 125-26.

4 Ibid.

5 Claude-François Achard, *Description historique, géographique et topographique des villes … de la Provence ancienne et moderne* 2 vols. (Aix-en-Provence, 1787); Abbé Paul de Grégoire, *Explication des cérémonies de la Fête-Dieu d'Aix-en-Provence* (Aix-en-Provence, 1777).

6 Michel Vovelle, "Apogée ou declin d'une capitale provinciale: le XVIIIe siècle," in Marcel Bernos, et al., *Histoire d'Aix-en-Provence* (Aix-en-Provence, 1977), p. 220, recounts these rumours.

7 Serge Conard, "Aux sources de l'architecture parlante, l'archéologie mystique de C.-N. Ledoux," in *Colloque Piranesi e la cultura antiquaria* (Rome, 1979), pp. 231-46; Jules-François Paul de Fauris de Saint-Vincens, *Mémoire pour remettre à Monseigneur l'archevêque d'Aix pour presser la reconstruction du palais*, 6 February 1784, in Gloton and Conard, "Aix-en-Provence," p. 60, and idem., *Mémoire sur le tour du Mausolée autrefois incorporée dans le Palais démoli en 1786*, Bibliothèque Méjanes, MS 1010, pp. 86-102; *Esprit Gibelin, Lettre sur les tours antiques qu'on a démolies à Aix-en-Provence* (Aix-en-Provence, 1787).

8 Charles-François Bouche, *Essai sur l'histoire de Provence*, 2 vols. (Marseille, 1785); idem., "Discours sur l'état actuel de la Provence," Introduction to Achard, *Description historique*, vol. 1, pp. 41-45.

9 Ledoux to Joseph Saveur Mignard, 14 November 1786, published in Léon de Berluc-Pérussis, "L'architecte Ledoux et le sculpteur Chardigny à Aix: Documents inédits (1776-1803), *Réunion des Sociétés des beaux-arts des départements* 26-27 (1902), pp. 189-225.

10 See Sharon Kettering, *Judicial Politics*, op. cit.

11 Da Sangallo's hypothetical reconstruction of 1496 is illustrated in Michel Clerc, *Aquae Sextiae: Histoire d'Aix-en-Provence dans l'antiquité* (Paris, 1910), pp. 430-31.

12 Blondel, *Cours*, II, p. 626.

13 Jacques-Pierre Brissot de Warville, *Théorie des lois criminelles* 2 vols.(Paris, 1781), I, pp. 183-185.

14 Pierre-Claude-Jean Tournatoris (1730-after 1794) collected anatomical specimens and was often attacked for his experiments in dissection. See Félix Chavernac, *Le docteur Tornatoris, sa vie et ses manuscrits* (Marseille, 1871).

15 See Ledoux, *L'Architecture*, p. 119. The ancient art of interpreting physiognomical evidence revived in popularity in the middle of the eighteenth century, supported by the publication of Johann Caspar Lavater's *Physiognomische Fragmente* (1775), later translated into French as *Essai sur la physionomie destiné à faire connoistre l'homme et à le faire aimer*, 4 vols. (Paris and the Hague, 1781-1803).

16 Conard, "Aux sources de l'architecture parlante," op. cit.

17 Charles Blanc, *Grammaire des arts du dessin: Architecture* (Paris, 1862), pp. 33-34.

9. FROM TOLLGATES TO PROPYLAEA

1 See E. Frémy, "L'enceinte de Paris, construit par les fermiers généraux et la perception des droits d'octroi de la ville (1784-1791)," *Bulletin de l'histoire de Paris et de l'Ile de France* 39 (1912), pp. 115-48.

2 Roger Dion, *Histoire de la vigne et du vin en France des origines au XIXe siècle* (Paris, 1959), especially pp. 505-31.

3 Laugier, *Essai sur L'Architecture*, p. 214.

4 Ibid.

5 Frémy, "L'enceinte de Paris," pp.117-118.

6 For a complete iconography of the barrières see Gallet, *Ledoux*, and especially Rabreau, *Ledoux*, pp. 235-274.

7 For a consistent depiction of the built *barrières* see Gaitte, *Receuil des plus belles maisons et des plus belles édifices de Paris* (Paris, c. 1792).

8 Report, 6 August 1786, Archives Nationales, T705 Colonia.

9 Report of 10 November 1785, Archives Nationales, T 705, Colonia.

10 See Dominique Poulot, "Modelli d'architettura," *Lotus International* 35 (1982), pp. 32-35.

11 See Thomas Brennan, "Beyond the Barriers: Popular Culture and Parisian *Guinguettes*," *Eighteenth-Century Studies* 18, No. 2 (Winter, 1984-85), pp. 153-69.

10. PHYSIOCRATIC REGIONALISM

1 Léon Four, *Le long des routes de Franche-Comté au XVIIIe siècle* (Besançon, 1935).

2 Bertrand's project was published in *Projet d'un canal de navigation pour joindre le Doubs à La Saône* (Besançon, 1777), quoted in Four, p. 107.

3 Pierre Pinon, et al., *Un canal, des canaux* (Paris, 1986), p. 343.

4 J.P. Ferrier, *Le duc de Choiseul, Voltaire et la création de Versoix-la-Ville, 1766-1777* (Geneva, 1922); André Corboz, *Invention de Carouge 1772-1792* (Lausanne, 1968).

5 Bibliothèque nationale de France, Paris, Ge. C9779. This plan was studied by Wolfgang Hermann in 1960 ("The Problem of Chronology in Ledoux's Engraved Work," *Art Bulletin* 41 (September, 1960), pp. 191-210) but dismissed

as too small in scale to have formed the basis for the later engraved "Carte des environs de la saline de Chaux." Yet a closer look reveals almost every aspect of the engraved topography, adjusted for further idealisation in the "Carte."

6 See J.-M. Pérouse de Monclos, *Les prix de Rome* (Paris, 1984).

7 For a succinct description of Physiocratic history and theory see Georges Weulersse, *La physiocratie sous les ministères de Turgot et Necker (1774-1781)* (Paris, 1950).

8 See Christian Devillers and Bernard Huet, *Le Creusot* (Seyssel, 1981).

11. AGRONOMIC ARCHITECTURE

1 The most complete account of the movement is André J. Bourde, *Agronomie et agronomes en France au XVIIIe siècle* 3 vols. (Paris, 1967).

2 The Duc de Béthune-Charost, of Meilhan in the Berry, was an agronomist, incarcerated with Ledoux under the Terror, and opened a rural school (for which Ledoux provided a design) in 1794.

3 François Cointeraux, *École d'architecture rurale* (Paris, 1791); and see Paolo Morachielle and Georges Teyssot, "La colonizzazione del territorio nel primo impero," *Lotus International* 24 (1979), pp. 24-39.

4 Engraving in the Archives du Département du Val de Marne, Melun.

5 For a description of the inhabitants of the forest, see M. Devèze, *La vie de la forêt française au XVI siècle* (Paris, 1961); Bourde, *Agronomie*, I, pp. 143ff; Lacroix, *La saline d'Arc-et-Senans*, pp. 66-78.

6 See *Actes du colloque sur la forêt* (Besançon 1966) (Paris, 1967), and Desiré Monnier, *Souvenirs d'un octogénaire de province, 1867-69* (Lons-le-Saunier, 1871).

7 Robert Mandrou, *De la culture populaire en France aux XVIIe et XVIIIe siècles* (Paris, 1964).

12. TEMPLES OF SOCIABILITY

1 Anthony Vidler, "The Architecture of the Lodges," op. cit.; Pierre Chevalier, *Histoire de la franc-maçonnerie française* (Paris, 1974).

2 For a list of orthodox freemasons in the lodges of the Grand Orient, see A. Le Bihan, *Francs-maçons parisiens du Grand Orient de France* 3 vols. (Paris, 1966).

3 J.W. Oliver, *The Life of William Beckford* (London, 1932), pp. 172-81.

4 Women were not admitted as members of the regular lodges, but formed "lodges of adoption" of their own after the 1770s.

13. UTOPIA OR REVOLUTION

1 Comité Révolutionnaire, Section de Faubourg du Nord, "Tableau des détenus," Archives Nationales, F7. 4774.11. This police dossier includes the record of arrest, the interrogation, Ledoux's own pleas for release, for permission to visit his house to fetch drawing and writing materials, letters from his daughters, and unfinished mémoires outlining his case for unpaid fees, etc.

2 "Demandes en liberté," Archives Nationales, F7.4774.11.

3 Ledoux to Joseph Saveur Mignard, 28 March, 1803, in Berluc-Pérussis, "L'architecte Ledoux," p. 219.

4 "Précis de l'ouvrage de Ledoux," and Letter of 20 Fructidor Year IX, in H. Ottomeyer, "Autobiographies d'architectes parisiens, 1759-1811," *Bulletin de la Société de l'histoire de Paris, 1971* (Paris, 1974), pp. 180-81.

5 De Choiseul-Gouffier, in Jacques Delille, *Oeuvres complètes* (Paris, 1852), p. 189. M. de Choiseul-Gouffier in writing the notes to part V of Delille's poem composed a eulogy to friendship, and to Ledoux's imaginary city. Delille's own tribute to "architecture" in the poem mentioned only two architects – Michelangelo and Ledoux. Ledoux himself had equally honored Delille in his design for the House of a Poet, as well as echoing the poet's translations of Virgil's *Aenead* and *Georgics*.

6 Paul V. Turner, "Claude-Nicolas Ledoux and the *Hypnerotomachia Poliphili*," unpublished (Stanford, 1996), p. 2. I believe that this note was prepared for a review of Ledoux and his work after his death, perhaps even for a eulogy at his funeral. Bélanger was the last friend to invite Ledoux to dinner three months before his death, an invitation that Ledoux, already ill, had to decline. The *Hypnerotomachia* was first published in Venice in 1499 and translated (much abridged) into French with revised engravings by Jean Martin, *Le songe de Poliphile* (Paris, 1546).

7 Ibid.

8 See Charles Ephrussi, *Etude sur Le songe de Poliphile* (Paris: Léon Techener, 1888), p.13. This study evokes the fin-de-siècle revival of interest in Renaissance humanism. For a publication history of the *Hypnerotomachia* see Gilles Polizzi, "Présentation," in Francesco Colonna, *Le songe de Poliphile* (Paris: Imprimerie Nationale, 1994), in particular pp.vii-xliv for the most important recent summary of the reception and translation of the *Hypnerotomachia*. This edition of the Jean Martin translation is also the most accurate scholarly edition to date. I am indebted to Dr Polizzi for a number of illuminating comments and corrections on this subject. There is a recent English translation by Joscelyn Godwin, *Hypnerotomachia Poliphili. The Strife of Love in a Dream* (London, 1999).

9 Ledoux is mentioned as a member of the Athénée des Etrangers, meeting in the former Hôtel Thélusson, from 1798-99 (*Veillée de Muses*, X, 1798 (vend. an VII). Members included: Brongniart, Ledoux, Legrand, and Pérard de Montreuil. The *Journal des arts, des sciences et de la littérature*, No. 277, 5 Prairial, an XI, [1803], p. 307, mentions a Société Philotechnique, with its secretary Lavallée; "cette société est autant au-dessus des Athénées qui pullulent dans Paris" and notes the reading of Legrand's translation of *Le songe de Poliphile*.

10 Jacques-Guillaume Legrand, *Le songe de Poliphile, traduction libre de l'italien*, 2 vols. (Paris, 1804). Legrand added a preface to a second edition (Parma, 1811). All citations from Legrand's 1811 edition will be in the form LH followed by the page number.

11 As noted, Charles-Alexandre de Calonne, Controller-General from 1784-1787, was a strong partisan of Ledoux; de Colonia was the primary official of the Ferme Générale in charge of the administration of the *barrières*. And while there are many debates over the authorship of the *Hypnerotomachia* the name "Francesco Colonna" spelled out by the chapter headings has remained convincing.

12 Pierre-Athanase Détournelle, Review of *L'Architecture*, in *Journal des arts, des sciences et de la littérature*, nos 340-344 (Paris, 1804); Anonymous reviewer, *Journal des monuments et des arts* (Paris, 1804)

CHRONOLOGY

Unless indicated otherwise, locations with street names are in Paris.

1736
Claude-Nicolas Ledoux born on 27th March at Dormans, Marne, France.

1749-53
Studies at the Collège de Beauvais, Paris.

1753-58
Studies at the École des Arts of Jacques-François Blondel, Paris.

1762
Decoration of the Salle de Café, Café Militaire, rue Saint-Honoré.

1763-66
Château de Maupertuis including the orangery, pheasantry, chapel, service buildings, pavilions for the agricultural guards and the concierge, plantation of the park, for the Marquis de Montesquiou.

1764-67
Château de Montfermeil (reconstruction), Seine-Saint-Denis, for the Président Jean-Hyacinthe-Louis-Emmanuel Hocquart; Pavilion Hocquart, rue Saint-Lazare and Chaussée d'Antin. Work for the Service des Eaux et Forêts: Rolampont, Neuilly-l'Evêque, Corgirnon, Culmont, Marac (Haute-Marne), Fouvent-le-Châtel, Roche-sur-Vannon (Haute-Saône), Villadin, Rigny-le-Feron (Aube), Cruzy-le-Châtel (Yonne).
Marries Marie Bureau, daughter of the royal musician, Joseph-Gaspard Bureau.

1765
Château de Brienon-l'Archevêque (Yonne) for the Cardinal de Luynes; Abbey of Escharlys, Villefranche (Yonne), cloister and front court. Project for an organ loft, cathedral of Auxerre.

1766
Hôtel d'Hallwyl, rue Michel-le-Comte, for Franz-Joseph d'Hallwyl, colonel in the Swiss Guards.
Maison Foucault, rue Basse-de-Rempart, for the Marquise de Foucault.
Apartment, Place Vendôme, for the Baron Crozat de Thiers.

1767
Unsuccessful canditature for the Académie d'Architecture.

1768
Hôtel d'Uzès, rue Montmartre, for François-Emmanuel de Crussol, Ninth Duke d'Uzès.

1769
Hôtel de Montmorency, Chaussée d'Antin, for Louis-François Joseph, Prince de Montmorency.
Project for Hôtel de Gourges, for Madame de Gourges, sister of the Président Chrétien-François II de Lamoignon.
Pavilion Saint-Germain, rue Saint-Lazare, for Louise Tirmant de Saint-Germain.

1770
Pavilion for the poet Saint-Lambert, Eaubonne, on the property of Joseph-Florent Le Normand de Mézières.
Château de Bénouville, near Caen, for Hippolyte-François Sanguin, Marquis de Livry.
Hôtel and Théâtre Guimard, Chaussée d'Antin, for Marie Madeleine Guimard, dancer at the Opéra.
Pavilion of Louveciennes, for Madame du Barry.

1771
Birth of daughter, Adélaïde-Constance.
Hôtel Tabary, rue du Faubourg Poissonnière for Pierre-René de Tabary.
Inaugural fête at Louveciennes (2 September). Ledoux named Commissaire aux Salines de Franche-Comté, Lorraine and Trois-Évêchés, adjunct to Perronet (20 September).

1772
Hôtel des équipages, Versailles, for Madame du Barry.
Inaugural performance in the Théâtre Guimard (8 December).

1773
Palace of Louveciennes for Madame du Barry.
Ledoux attains a Second Class membership in the Académie d'Architecture.
Studies for the feasibility of the Saline near Arc-et-Senans (Order in Council, April 23).
First project for the Saline de Chaux.

1774
Contract for the building of the Saline de Chaux signed between the Ferme Générale and Jean Roux Monclar, entrepreneur of Paris (12 March, to take effect October).
Surveys of site for Saline de Chaux (14 September).
Second project for the Saline de Chaux sent to the site engineer (28 October, described as the "plan de masse").

1775
Final selection of site for Saline de Chaux (January).
Construction of Saline de Chaux authorised by Royal Order (14 February).
Foundation stone of Saline de Chaux laid (15 April).
Commission for Theatre of Besançon from the Intendant of Franche-Comté, Charles-André de Lacoré.
Ledoux sends detailed plan of the first floor of the Saline de Chaux to the site (2 June).
Ledoux sends elevations for Saline de Chaux (16 June).
Birth of second daughter, Alexandrine-Euphrasie.
First project for Theatre of Besançon (25 August).
Hôtel de Cramayel, rue du Sentier, for François Fontaine de Cramayel, Farmer General.
Grenier à sel Compiègne, for the Ferme Générale.
Travels to Germany and visits Hesse-Cassel (December).
Project for Triumphal Arch, Cassel.
Project for Château Saint-Vrain, for Madame du Barry.

1776
Project for Museum Fredericianum, or Library of Cassel.
Visit to Aix-en-Provence to survey old Palais de Justice.

1778
Hôtel Thélusson, rue de Provence, for Marie-Jeanne Thélusson, widow of the banker Tobie Thélusson.
Project for a Hunting Lodge, Scey-sur-Saône, for the prince Charles-Roger de Bauffremont-Listenois.

1779
Theatre of Besançon

1779-83
Three projects for Palais de Justice, Aix-en-Provence.

1780
Project for Hôtel d'Artagnan de Fezensac de Montesquiou.
Hôtel d'Attilly (de Jarnac), Faubourg Poissonnière.
Hôtel d'Espinchal, rue des Petites-Écuries.
House for M. de Witt (project).

1783
Hôtel de Valentinois, rue Saint-Lazare.
Hôtel de la Ferme Générale, rue de Grenelle.

1784
Project for Hôtel de Ville, Neufchatel.
Project for Theatre, Marseille.
Calonne approves the plans for the wall of the Ferme Générale around Paris (11 June).

1784-85
Projects for Palais de Justice and prison, Aix-en-Provence.

1785-1789
Barrières of Paris for the Ferme Générale.
Projects for Maison de commerce, rue Saint-Denis; Village of Maupertuis; Caisse d'Escompte; Maisons Saisseval; maison rue Neuve de Berry; Hôtel d'Evry; Ferme, rue Saint-Lazare; Château de Barrail; Château d'Eyguières; Episcopal Palace of Sisteron; Model Farm and Sheepfold, La Roche-Bernard; park and *fabriques*, Château de Bourneville; Governor's Palace, Aix-en-Provence.

1789
Engraving of first Frontispiece for *L'Architecture*.
Definitive suspension from work on the *barrières* (23 May).
Burning of the *barrières* (10-14 July).
Anonymous publication of *Un bonhomme aux Etats-généraux*, accusing Poyet of plagiarism.

1790
Project for a new Opéra presented to Commune de Paris.

1791
Suspension of works at Aix-en-Provence.

1792
Maisons Hosten, rue Saint-Georges, for J.B. Hosten.
Death of Marie-Bureau Ledoux.

1793
Arrest of Ledoux (29 November).

1794
Death of Adélaïde-Constance Ledoux.

1795
Release of Ledoux (13 January).
Project for the Rural School of Meilhan for the Duc de Béthune-Charost.

1800
"Précis de l'ouvrage de Ledoux architecte" deposited with the Institut.

1803
Prospectus for *L'Architecture*.

1804
L'Architecture consideree sous le rapport de l'art, des moeurs et de la legislation, Vol. I.

1806
Death of Ledoux (19 November).
Funeral of Ledoux, Cemetery of Montmartre (21 November), Paris.

BIBLIOGRAPHY

General

Actes du colloque "Piranèse et les Français," 12-14 May 1976, Rome, published under the direction of G. Brunel, Rome, 1978, collection of Académie de France in Rome.

Résumé du colloque Soufflot, colloque "Soufflot et l'architecture des lumières," Lyon, 1980.

J.D. Bandiera, "The city of the dead: French eighteenth-century design for funerary complexes," in Gazette des beaux-arts, 1983, 101, n° 1368, p. 25-32.

F. Benoît, L'Art français sous la Révolution et l'Empire, Paris, 1897.

M. Gallet, Demeures parisiennes à l'époque de Louis XVI, Paris, 1964.

E. Kaufmann, Architecture in the Age of Reason; Baroque and Post-Baroque in England, Italy, and France, Cambridge, 1955.

E. Kaufmann, "Architektonische Entwürfe aus der Zeit der französischen Revolution," Zeitschrift für bildende Kunst, 1929-1930.

E. Kaufmann, Die Krise der Baukunst um 1800, Stockholm, 1933.

E. Kaufmann, Von Ledoux bis Le Corbusier, Ursprung und Entwicklung der autonomen Architektur, Vienna, 1933.

H. Lipstadt, "Soufflot, De Wailly, Ledoux; la fortune critique dans la presse architecturale," 1800-1825, in Cahiers de la recherche architecturale, Paris, 1980, n° 6-7, pp. 298-303.

H. Rosenau, The Ideal City in Its Architectural Evolution, London, 1959.

J. Starobinski, Les Emblèmes de la raison, Paris, 1973.

B. Stoloff, S. Ziegler, L'Architecte sous l'Ancien Régime, Association pour la recherche près l'Institut d'architecture et d'urbanisme de Strasbourg, Strasbourg, 1978.

A.M. Vogt, Die Französische Revolutionarchitektur und der Newtonismus, Berlin, 1967.

Writings of Ledoux

C.N. Ledoux, Manuscrits, Archives nationales, T 705, Q1 1.101, Q1 1.933.

C.N. Ledoux, Prospectus to L'Architecture considérée sous le rapport de l'art, des mœurs, et de la législation, Paris, 1802. 2nd edition, Introduction A. Vidler, Arc-et-Senans, 1985.

C.N. Ledoux, L'Architecture considérée sous le rapport de l'art, des mœurs et de la législation, Paris, 1804.

C.N. Ledoux, L'Architecture de Claude-Nicolas Ledoux, 2 vol., edited and with a preface by D. Ramée, Paris, 1847. Facsimile of this edition, Princeton, 1984.

C.N. Ledoux, L'Architecture considérée sous le rapport de l'art, des mœurs et de la législation, anastatic edition by F. De Nobele, 2 vol., Paris, 1962.

C.N. Ledoux, L'Architecture considérée sous le rapport de l'art, des mœurs et de la législation, vol. 1, New York, 1980, facsimile of the Paris edition, 1804.

C.N. Ledoux, L'Architecture considérée sous le rapport de l'art, des mœurs et de la législation, Nördlingen, 1981, facsimile of the Paris edition, 1804.

C.-N. Ledoux, L'Architecture considérée sous le rapport de l'art, des moeurs et de la législation, Paris, Hermann, 1997.

C.-N. Ledoux, Architecture Considered in Relation to Art, Mores, and Legislation. A Critical Edition, trans. Anthony Vidler and Rodolphe el Khoury, New York, forthcoming, 2005-6.

Ledoux, Architect and Theoretician

M. Brion, "Un précurseur de l'architecture moderne," in Beaux Arts, January 1937.

Y. Christ, L. Schein, L'Œuvre et les rêves de Claude-Nicolas Ledoux, Paris, 1971.

Y. Christ, Projets et divagations de Claude-Nicolas Ledoux, Paris, 1961.

S. Conard, "Aux sources de l'architecture parlante. L'archéologie mystique de C.N. Ledoux". Symposium Presentation "Piranesi e la cultura antiquaria," Rome, 1979.

S. Cordier, La Séduction du merveilleux. C.N. Ledoux, E.L. Boullée, J.J. Lequeu, Aix-en-Provence, 1968.

M. Gallet, "La jeunesse de Ledoux," in Gazette des beaux-arts, February 1970, pp. 65-92.

M. Gallet, "Ledoux et sa clientèle parisienne," in Bulletin de la Société de l'histoire de Paris, 1974-1975, pp. 131-173.

M. Gallet, Claude-Nicolas Ledoux (1736-1809), Paris, 1980.

M. Gallet, Architecture de C.-N. Ledoux. Inédits pour un tome III, Paris, 1991.

K. Gallwitz, G. Metken, Revolutionsarchitektur, Boullée, Ledoux, Lequeu, Baden-Baden, 1974.

H. Graham, "Ledoux and his Ideal City," in Apollo, November 1963.

W. Hermann. "The problem of chronology in Claude-Nicolas Ledoux's engraved work," in Art Bulletin, September 1960, vol. XLII, 3.

E. Kaufmann, "Die Stadt des Architekten Ledoux," in Kunstwissenschaftliche Forschungen, 1932, II.

E. Kaufmann, "C.N. Ledoux, inaugurator of a new architectural system," in Journal of the Society of Architectural Historians, 1944, IV, 2.

E. Kaufmann, Three Revolutionary Architects, Boullée, Ledoux and Lequeu, Philadelphia, 1952.

J. Langner, Claude-Nicolas Ledoux. Die erste Schaffenszeit 1762-1774, S.L. 1959.

J. Langner, "Ledoux und die "Fabriques". Voraussetzungen der Revolutionsarchitektur im Landschaftsgarten," in Zeitschrift für Kunstgeschichte, 1963, 1, pp. 1-36.

D. Le Comte, Boullée, Ledoux, Lequeu: les architectes révolutionnaires, Paris, 1969.

J.C. Lemagny, Visionary Architects: Boullée, Ledoux, Lequeu, University of St. Thomas, Houston, 1968.

G. Levallet-Haug, Claude-Nicolas Ledoux 1736-1806, Paris-Strasbourg, 1934.

G. Levallet-Haug, "Un projet d'urbanisme au XVIIIe siècle," Urbanisme, 1935.

R. Middleton, "The Château and Gardens of Maupertuis. The Formal and the Informal," in Garden History. Issues, Approaches, Methods, ed. J. Dixon Hunt, Washington, D.C., 1992.

J.C. Moreux, M. Raval, Claude-Nicolas Ledoux, architecte du roi, Paris.

M. Ozouf, "L'image de la ville chez Claude-Nicolas Ledoux," in Annales, économie, société, civilisation, November-December 1966.

D. Rabreau, "Nature et architecture parlante: Soufflot, De Wailly et Ledoux touchés par les lumières," in Résumé du colloque Soufflot, Lyon, 1980.

D. Rabreau, Claude-Nicolas Ledoux (1736-1806). L'Architecture et les fastes du temps, Paris, William Blake et Co., 2000.

D. Rabreau, La Saline Royale d'Arc-et-Senans. Un monument industriel allégorie des lumières, Paris, 2002.

J. Rittaud-Hutinet, La Vision d'un futur: Ledoux et ses théâtres, Lyon, 1982.

H. Rosenau, "Claude-Nicolas Ledoux," in Burlington Magazine, 1946, LXXX-VIII.

H. Rosenau, "Boullée and Ledoux as towns planners a re-assessment," in Gazette des beaux-arts, 1964, pp. 173-190.

H. Rosenau, "Ledoux, an essay in historiography," in Gazette des beaux-arts, 1983, 101, n° 1372-1373, pp. 177-186.

M. Saboya, "Claude-Nicolas Ledoux et son utopie sociale," in Information d'histoire de l'art, 1970, n° 3, pp. 136-138.

B. Stoloff, L'Affaire Claude-Nicolas Ledoux: autopsie d'un mythe, Bruxelles, 1977.

A. Vidler, Claude-Nicolas Ledoux. Architecture and Social Reform at the End of the Ancien Régime, Cambridge, Mass., MIT Press, 1990.

INDEX OF PERSONS